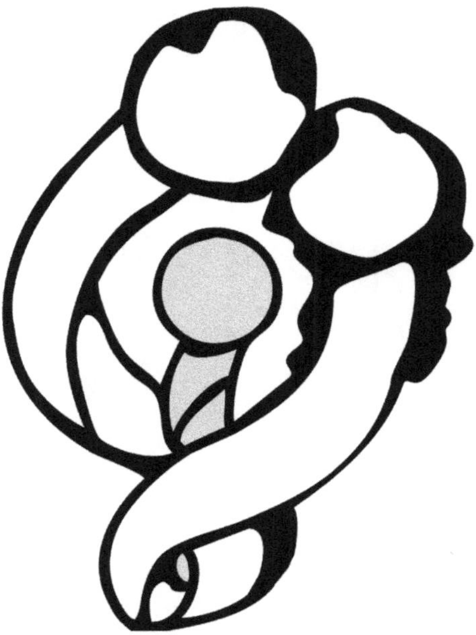

The essential book for anyone at the crossroads of parenthood — clear, compassionate, and courageously honest.

PSYCHOTHERAPIST
CRISTINA NICA

WHY DO WE REALLY WANT A BABY?

— FROM REASONS TO CONSEQUENCES —

LETRAS
Promovăm autorii români

CIP description of the National Library of Romania
NICA, CRISTINA
Why Do We Really Want a Baby? From reasons to consequences / Cristina Nica – Otopeni: Letras, 2026
Includes bibliography
ISBN 978-630-312-638-8

159.9

ISBN eBook ePUB: 978-630-312-639-5

Print on Demand

Book distributed by www.piatadecarte.net
email: office@piatadecarte.com.ro
Orders: +40 748 126 309 // +40 787 708 844

For publishing inquiries, please contact the publishing house at: edituraletras@piatadecarte.com.ro

Letras Publishing House / www.letras.ro
contact@letras.ro

Contents

Preface

Of the courage to gaze beyond desire

Cristina Nica's book is read with the mind and felt with the heart. It is an invitation into the deepest reaches of the soul and thought, where we meet our inner truth—sometimes uncomfortable, other times painful. Cristina leads us beyond the boundaries of social conventions and stereotypes, beyond convenient justifications and motivations, to the place where the questions that change us begin.

She addresses one of the most sensitive subjects, which for centuries we have lived through in unquestioned conformity, as if it were an untouchable truth. Having children was considered a duty, a natural life path for everyone, rather than a conscious choice. Cristina has the courage to open this subject with gentleness and lucidity, inviting us to look into the depths of our hidden motives.

This book is extremely valuable for those who are not yet parents—a call for honesty, authenticity, and responsibility toward the life we may bring into the world. But it is equally important for those who are already parents: even if the decision to have a child was made from a less conscious place, Cristina offers landmarks through which the bond with the child can be reorganized, healed, and refreshed by authentic love.

The book does not speak of the perfection of being a parent, but of truth—of our human fragility, of the fears that hide beneath love, and of the courage to acknowledge our limits. Within its pages, parenthood becomes a journey back to authenticity—a path where the child is not a mirror of our own voids, but a free being, worthy of being loved for who they are.

There are pages that hurt, but also heal. Words that reveal, but also soothe. Cristina Nica writes with a tender clarity, with empathy and the lucidity of a therapist who has spent a long time in the presence of human pain without judging it.

I read this book with the emotion of recognition. In its pages, I found the questions I have heard so many times in the therapeutic space—questions about meaning, love, and freedom. And if you have reached the final page, you may already feel that the journey is not over. The true question is only just beginning: **"How can I love without fear?"**

This, I believe, is the silent legacy of Cristina Nica's book —the courage to choose conscious love, not as a reaction, but as a gift.

CRISTINA SCHMIDT

Transgenerational Psychotherapist

Associate Professor, Faculty of Psychology and Educational Sciences

Vice-President Institute of Transgenerational Studies and Practices

Chair of International Committee ASGPP (American Association for Group Psychotherapy and Psychodrama)

Recipient of the Zerka Moreno Award (2024)

Foreword

To the mothers who wonder if they are enough, to those who carry the fear of being judged: never forget that a child born and raised in love does not overshadow the journey, but opens another path toward fulfillment!

Before there was US,

There was first ME.

But perhaps never complete,

For no one told me I had so many choices to make.

I felt I would be judged,

That I was too much or too little,

Only that I long to hear your crystal laughter,

Your divine scent of milk,

And even the cries in the dead of night.

I feared I would fail at motherhood,

That I would lose my identity,

But from all these worries I created a new reality,

In which I withdrew from captivity

And surprisingly succeeded in dividing my heart in two

And yet becoming new.
My children have shown me many answers,
But undoubtedly it would have been encouraging
To have a book like this
For more clarity.

— Gabriela Negoiță

Chapter 1

Why was this book written?

This book was not written out of a sudden impulse, but out of an accumulation—of observations and knowledge. Over the years, I have noticed and witnessed unspoken questions and subtle pains that lingered in my mind after every conversation with an exhausted mother, an absent father, or a child who doesn't understand why they are never 'enough.'

For a long time, I have looked around and seen children carrying burdens that do not belong to them. Children brought into this world as solutions, shields, or rescue projects. Children growing up in the absence of authentic love, yet in the presence of suffocating expectations.

I see parents who have never asked themselves *why* they want a child. Those who have confused desire with need, love with fear, and maturity with conformity.

I see adults living out their own unlived childhoods through their children. Those who follow the principle: 'If I didn't have it, my child should.' Those who see a chance to finish a degree, for instance, through their child, because they couldn't do it in their time. I see adults who project, repeat, and transfer.

And I see children growing up with wounds that are invisible to some, yet deep. Wounds that do not heal with age but transform into patterns, blockages—in other words, into silent suffering. I see children crying out for love and attention, wanting to learn from their own mistakes, wanting to carve their own path in life, yet growing up according to templates.

Society teaches us that the desire to have children is natural, instinctive, and universal. But what happens when instinct is distorted by trauma, pressure, or the need to belong? What happens when 'having a child' becomes a checkmark on a life list, rather than a conscious choice?

I have felt, more and more acutely, that children around me are being born for the wrong reasons. Not morally wrong, but wrong because they are unconscious.

I started writing because I have seen too many unhappy people who do not know how to manage their sadness, pain, frustration, and unfulfillment.

For future parents, the motivation often hides behind phrases like 'it's time,' 'the biological clock is ticking,' or 'it's just what you do'—yet beneath these, there may lie an untold, painful story.

I wrote this for the woman who feels guilty for not feeling the maternal instinct. For the man who doesn't know if his desire for a child stems from love, from a need to feel whole, or from a desire to please his parents. For the couple wondering if a child will save their relationship. For those who choose not to have children and are sometimes viewed as 'outcasts.' Because bringing a life into this world is not merely a biological act, but an act of conscience and responsibility.

This book is a campaign, if you will—a call to awareness, an invitation to introspection. It is not about parenting, but about *pre-parenting*. It is about that moment of absolute honesty when we ask ourselves:

– Am I ready to become a parent?

– What truly motivates me?

– What emotional baggage am I carrying?

– What kind of world do I want to create for my child?

– What expectations do I have of my child?

If we do not ask ourselves these questions, we risk bringing children into this world who will become lost adults—lost in their thoughts, negative beliefs, emotions, relationships, professions, and in life itself. And we, as future parents, risk losing ourselves in this role, seeing the raising and education of our children as an eternal sacrifice. However, it is far more rewarding to walk the path accompanied by someone than to feel like you are carrying them on your back for a lifetime.

This book is not a guide; it does not tell you what to do. But it makes you pay attention to the consequences—something that applies to every family member involved.

This book does not judge, yet it does not coddle either. It challenges you and holds up mirrors. It opens uncomfortable conversations and offers you a space to truly listen to yourself.

If you are reading these lines, it means you are searching for answers, and that, in itself, is an act of courage.

And if we do not start talking about this subject, we will carry on to repeat the same mistakes. In silence, out of both love and ignorance.

Chapter 2

Why do we choose to become parents?

„Children don't need perfect parents.
They need authentic parents".
Gabor Maté

The decision to become a parent is, perhaps, one of the most intimate and complex choices a human being can make. Although in contemporary society it is often presented as a natural stage —a "normal" step in the evolution of life—in reality, this choice is profoundly influenced by a multitude of factors: some conscious, others subtle, hidden within the deep layers of our psyche. Becoming a parent is not merely a biological decision, but an existential one, involving a redefinition of the self, a shift in roles, and a responsibility that spans decades.

In the past, having children was a necessity—a guarantee of family survival, a form of insurance for old age, a religious obligation, a helping hand for household chores, or a duty to one's lineage. In traditional societies, fertility was celebrated, and motherhood was seen as a supreme virtue. Today, in the era of choice and individualism, the decision to become a parent is no longer dictated by external needs, but by an inner search—and that is precisely why it becomes more complex, more fragile, and more personal.

In this chapter, we will examine the four most frequent motivations underlying the decision to have a child: desire, meaning, the idea of continuity, and conscious choice. Each of these carries nuances, ramifications, and profound implications for how the parent-child relationship will be built.

A client once told me: *"I look around and see how all my friends have children. I feel strange that I don't have the same impulse. I wonder if there's something wrong with me or if, quite simply, it's just not the right time. I'd like us to go out more often, as we used to, but they are always busy with various activities for the kids or have no one to leave them with. At every meeting with my family of origin, my parents ask me when I will give them a grandchild. It's as if I wouldn't exist without the role of mother."*

If we pause for a moment on this account, we notice the weight of the story and the mission my client grew up with: that it isn't normal not to have children, as if something were broken within you; that it is a sign of selfishness not to sacrifice your life for your own children. And just like that, the belief takes root that "I am not good enough and perhaps I never will be." *How can I exist or be happy if I don't have children?*

But what happens when we choose to become parents not out of love, but out of fear? Not out of consciousness, but out of conformity? Not out of maturity, but out of a need to feel whole?

I remember a client who said: *"My wife has wanted a child for years. Me... I don't know. I'm terrified of the idea that I won't be a good father. That I'll repeat my father's mistakes that I won't have time for myself, for us. But at the same time, I think that maybe this is my chance to break the cycle, to do things differently. And yet, when will I know that I'm ready for this?"*

Let us settle for a moment on this account.

First, there is the fear of repeating certain family patterns —a central theme in transgenerational psychology. This was a theme my client brought into therapy himself, rather than one identified as a new observation following the drafting of the genogram. The man fears becoming a copy of his father, which suggests that his relationship with the paternal figure was marked by pain, absence, or dysfunctional behaviors. This fear indicates an awareness of trauma, but also a desire to overcome it. He is not running from the past; he views it with lucidity, which is a sign of psychological maturation.

Next, the conflict between the desire for autonomy and relational responsibility takes shape. *"To have time for myself, for us"* expresses the need for personal space, for freedom, and for maintaining an individual identity within the couple. This is a legitimate concern, especially since the arrival of a child can radically transform the dynamics of a relationship. This part of the phrase suggests that the man is not only concerned with the role of father, but also with maintaining balance in the couple's relationship—a sign that he does not see the child as a "salvific glue," but as a challenge to be embraced by both partners. I believe it is wonderful not to lose ourselves in a single social role, but rather to support our entire lives on as many pillars as possible.

At the same time, an emotional ambivalence emerges: fear and hope. *"Maybe this is my chance to break the cycle"* is an extremely powerful statement. It indicates a deep motivation—not just to become a father, but to transform a painful legacy into an act of healing and reparation. It is the voice of a man who does not want to repeat, but to rewrite—to give a positive connotation to a story already written. This intention is essential in the process of conscious parenting: *I already know how my father behaved toward me; I wish to become a much better version of him, keeping what I liked and what did me good, while eliminating and transforming what I no longer like.*

Finally, the question *"And yet, when will I know that I'm ready for this?"* is an existential one. It expresses identity uncertainty, the fear of failure, but also the need for validation. In psychotherapy, such questions do not have absolute answers; instead, they become starting points for exploration. Readiness does not come from a magic moment, but from a process of commitment, of learning, and of accepting imperfection.

This entire passage is an example of emotional consciousness in the making. It is not the voice of an unprepared man, but of a man who is preparing—through reflection, through fear, and through hope. And it is precisely this honesty that brings him closer to a conscious choice.

In conclusion, becoming a parent is not a simple "check-off" on a predetermined path. It is a choice born from a mixture of desire, fear, personal history, and projections of the future. For some, it is a profound calling. For others, a question without a clear answer. And for many, a decision that transforms over time, as wounds heal, needs are clarified, and identity is redefined.

In therapy, the question *"Do I really want to be a parent?"* has no universal answer. But it holds immense value simply because it is asked. It opens doors to the self, to the relationship with parents, with the partner, and with the future. It is a question that does not demand haste, but honesty. It does not demand perfection, but courage.

Regardless of the answer, the process of exploration is in itself a form of maturation. Because we are not just choosing whether to have a child; we are choosing what kind of people we want to be in the face of a decision that can profoundly transform us.

2.1. Desire

The desire to have a child is, on the surface, a natural impulse. It is often expressed through phrases like "I feel like I want a child," "I want to be a mother," or "I would like to have someone of my own." However, desire, in its raw form, is not always an indicator of a mature choice. It can be fueled by unfulfilled needs, social pressures, comparisons, or personal ideals.

Psychologically speaking, this desire can hide a need for validation, belonging, or unconditional love. Some people want a child because they feel that, in doing so, they will be loved, seen, and understood. Others want a child because they grew up with the idea that this is life's ultimate purpose. Desire can also be a reaction to loneliness, to the fear of growing old alone, or to the need for an external "meaning" to fill internal voids.

It is important to ask ourselves: what generates this desire? Is it an expression of emotional maturity or a form of compensation? Desire, in itself, is not wrong. But if it is not accompanied by reflection—by a deep understanding of the motives behind it—it can lead to impulsive decisions, projections onto the child, and strained relationships.

A child is not an answer to an unspoken question. They are not a bandage for an old wound. They are not a trophy, an achievement, or a guarantee of happiness. The desire to have a child needs to be coupled with the ability to see them as a separate being, with their own needs, dreams, and paths.

The desire to have children is not always born from a rational decision. Sometimes, it emerges as an inner whisper, a diffuse emotion that cannot be explained in words. It is a calling that creeps in during moments of vulnerability, in recurring dreams, or in questions that have no immediate answer. It is a desire nourished by many sources—some deeply rooted in biology, others in the soul, and others in the imagination.

The Biological Instinct – The instinct to perpetuate life is one of the oldest human impulses. It requires no moral or social justification. It manifests subtly: in the moments we see a child smile, when we feel an inexplicable void around young families, or when our bodies react to the fragility of a tiny being. It is a desire that demands no logic, only presence. In therapy, many discover that this calling does not stem from a conscious plan, but from a profound part of the self that seeks to leave a mark, to continue a story.

The Need for Unconditional Love – For some, the desire to have children is closely linked to the need to love and be loved in a pure way, unaltered by conditions or expectations. It is the dream of a relationship where affection is not negotiated but offered in abundance. In this vision, becoming a parent becomes a form of healing—an opportunity to experience a love that does not demand performance, but simply presence. Within this desire lies the hope that, through the child, a bond can be built to repair old wounds and bring a sense of meaning and belonging.

The Projection of an Ideal – For others, the desire to have children is tied to an idealized vision of life. The child becomes a symbol of continuity, of hope, and of the possibility of creating something better than what came before. It is a form of emotional activism—an attempt to pass down values, to build a fairer, gentler world in miniature. Sometimes, this desire comes from a place of pain: from lacks, from trauma, or from unfulfillment. Other times, it comes from a place of abundance: from the desire to share, to give, and to multiply the beauty one has experienced.

This desire, in all its forms, deserves to be explored with gentleness. It is neither good nor bad. It is a part of ourselves that calls for listening, not judgment. In therapy, it can be understood not just as a life choice, but as a window into the self—into what we lack, what we yearn for, what we fear, and what we hope for.

2.2. Meaning

For many people, a child becomes the meaning of life. They are seen as a justification for existence, a reason to live, a form of ultimate fulfillment. "My life has no meaning without a child," "I feel I must leave something behind," "I want to feel that I have done something important."

This motivation is profound and, at times, spiritual. Having a child is perceived as a connection to something greater than oneself. It is a desire to contribute, to create, to leave a mark. However, meaning is an internal construct. If we project it exclusively onto the child, we menace turning them into a symbol—a pure carrier of our own fulfillment.

In this way, the child becomes responsible for the parent's happiness. For their emotional balance. For the justification of their very existence. And when the child fails to meet these expectations, guilt, shame, and anxiety emerge. The child feels they must be "good," "successful," or "special" just so the parent can feel fulfilled.

The meaning of life cannot be delegated. It cannot be placed on the shoulders of a being who is just learning to walk, to take their first steps in life. Having a child can bring meaning, but it should not be the *only* source. It is essential for parents to construct their own sense of meaning, to heal their wounds, and to define their values before bringing into the world a life that will be shaped by all of these.

Personal fulfillment often stems from the feeling that life is taking on a new shape. A child does not fill a void; instead, they create a new dimension of existence. It is a redefinition of priorities—a maturation that is sometimes forced, yet beautiful.

However, this fulfillment is not about repairing something that is missing, but about adding something new and profound. Becoming a parent is not an act of completion, but rather one of transformation. It is not like adding a missing piece to the puzzle of existence; it is like redrawing the entire map of one's life.

Many believe that a child "heals" loneliness or unfulfillment, but the truth is that they bring challenges that demand a solid identity. A child does not fill; they challenge. It is as if you want to build a house without checking the ground first. What do you do if the ground is a marshland?

Responsibility Toward the World – This can be a motivation for some who choose to become parents. Why? Because they feel they can contribute to a better society. Through education, care, and the example they set, they hope to leave behind not just a life, but an influence. Thus, parenthood becomes not only a personal choice but also a form of social commitment.

Some people feel they can positively influence the world through the way they raise their children. In this sense, education, care, love, and personal example become valuable tools for shaping the future. The idea of "leaving something behind," in this context, refers not just to genes, but to values and attitudes.

Inner transformation is inevitable. It doesn't happen overnight or at the snap of a fingers. Being a parent isn't just a change in daily routine; it is, rather, a profound transformation of the human being.

Children teach us patience, challenge our limits, and, in a way, force us to be present. They become mirrors in which we see ourselves more clearly, more honestly, and more vulnerably. Why? Because they are demanding, and they aren't born with a "preset" to respect their parents' rhythm. Everything becomes like a dance: sometimes we slow down, other times we pick up the pace; we learn to listen, to just be there. As for boundaries, they are constantly tested; likely starting from the moment those two lines appear on a pregnancy test. Sleep and personal space undergo significant changes. And if we truly listen, perhaps over time, we notice that it is the child who reflects our emotions, tensions, and joy—teaching us to let go of what doesn't matter and urging us toward continuous growth.

2.3. Continuity

The idea of continuity is one of the oldest motivations for having children. The desire to pass on genes, names, values, and traditions —all of these are part of the instinct for perpetuation. Thus, the child becomes an extension of the self, a form of immortality, a bridge between generations. It is the desire to carry on a story.

This motivation can be beautiful if it is accompanied by respect for the child's individuality. However, it often transforms into a subtle form of control. The parent projects their own unfulfilled dreams, ideals, and traumas onto the child. They see the child as an "heir" rather than a free being.

"I didn't manage to become a doctor, but my child will succeed." "I didn't get love, but my child will receive everything I didn't have." "I was humiliated, but my child will be respected." These statements, though they seem full of love, hide a dynamic of transfer and projection that can suffocate the child if we are not mindful of our emotional baggage and, perhaps, our balance.

Continuity should not be a copy. The child is not a copy, but a creation—a new life. They have the right to be different, to choose another path, and to reject parental values that do not suit them. True continuity is that which allows for evolution, not duplication. It is that which offers freedom, not constraint. It is that which encourages authenticity, not conformity.

2.4. Conscious Choice

In a world where social pressures, family expectations, and romantic ideals can influence personal decisions, it is vital to ask ourselves: “Are we taking this step because we truly want it, or because ‘that’s just what people do’?”

Conscious choice is, perhaps, the only motivation that does not involve projections, pressures, or unfulfilled needs. It is a decision made with maturity, introspection, and responsibility. It is the moment when a person honestly asks themselves: “Am I ready to be a parent?”, “What truly motivates me?”, “What emotional baggage am I carrying?”, “What kind of world do I want to create for my child?”

Making a conscious choice requires the courage to look inward, to recognize one’s own limits, and to accept that parenting is not about perfection, but about presence. It is a choice that does not stem from fear, pressure, or a desire to fix something, but from a place of mature love.

The conscious parent is not the one who knows everything, but the one who is willing to learn. Not the one who has all the answers, but the one who asks the right questions. Not the one who controls, but the one who accompanies. Not the one who assigns blame, but the one who seeks solutions. Conscious choice involves letting go of rigid ideals and projections, opening oneself to the living reality of the child, with all its imperfections and beauties.

It is a choice that comes after a period of introspection—a sincere analysis of one’s own childhood, the relationship with one’s parents, and inherited emotional and relational patterns. It is a choice that is not made in a hurry, nor out of fear or the desire to “not miss the boat.” It is a choice that requires the courage to say “not now” or even “maybe never” if the inner answers are not clear.

To be a conscious parent means accepting that you will make mistakes, that you will sometimes be overwhelmed, and that you will feel guilt, fatigue, and frustration. But it also means being present, being attentive, and being willing to repair, to learn, and to grow alongside your child. It is a form of mature love that does not demand perfection, but authenticity.

In a conscious choice, there are no guarantees. There are no promises that everything will be easy or beautiful. However, there is a solid foundation, a clear intention, and an emotional availability that can make the difference between raising a child and molding them according to one's own needs. It is the difference between accompanying and leading, between listening and imposing, between loving and conditioning.

This choice is rarely discussed in the public sphere. There is much talk about parenting, methods, and styles, but too little about "moment zero"—that point of absolute honesty where a person asks: "Why do I want a child?" Conscious choice begins there. In the silence between thoughts. In the courage not to run away from uncomfortable answers. In the desire not to repeat, but to transform.

Chapter 3

Unhealthy Motivation 1: Out of Fear of Loneliness or as Support in Old Age

---

„When the child becomes the parent's rescue project, love turns into obligation. And obligation kills freedom."
Alice Miller

In a world where individualism is on the rise and relationships are becoming increasingly fluid and fragile, the fear of loneliness creeps into many people's lives. For some, this fear becomes so overwhelming that it influences major life decisions, including the choice to have children.

There is a heavy silence surrounding this motivation. Few admit it out loud, but many carry it in their thoughts. The fear of loneliness is one of the most universal human fears. It disregards age, social status, or education. It is that void felt in moments of stillness —on evenings when no one asks, "How are you feeling?" or "How was your day?" In days when someone else's presence seems like the only guarantee that you exist.

For some, the idea of having a child becomes an antidote to this fear. A child who will be there, provide company, fill the house with noise, and bring meaning to moments of silence. Later, the child becomes the projection of an easier old age: someone who will care, visit, bring the proverbial glass of water, and hold one's hand in moments of helplessness. This is an image that, in our culture, has been passed down from generation to generation—like an unwritten debt, a form of balance between what you give and what you receive.

Yes, it is true—any relationship involves an exchange: you give something, you get something. I know, it sounds like a kind of unwritten contract between two parties, but that is the reality. Look at the relationships around you—friendships, romantic ties, extended family, or professional ones. The true imbalance in a relationship occurs when one gives far too much and receives too little. In that case, you have a choice: continue in the same cycle or reset your personal boundaries.

But this motivation, however natural it may seem, hides a dangerous dynamic. Because a child is not a guarantor of companionship, nor a social worker in the making. They are an autonomous being, with their own dreams, worries, and paths. Bringing them into the world with the hope that they will fill a void or support one's old age is a form of conditioning.

It is not said directly, but it is felt. The child grows up with the pressure not to move too far away, to be "grateful," and to "give back" what was offered. Of course, all sorts of ambivalent messages can be sent, such as: "You can go out with your friends, stay as long as you want, but be careful what time you come home!" What is a child to understand from this message: am I allowed to stay out as long as I want, or is my time limited?

In therapy, this theme emerges frequently: adults who feel guilty for not being "enough" for their parents. They feel obligated to stay close, to give up on their dreams, to provide care, to fix things, or to enter relationships—not because they want to, but because they were raised with the idea that "this is just how it's done." This belief is often stronger than their desire to change anything in their lives. They have learned that love is measured in sacrifice and that presence is an obligation, not a choice.

But love cannot be demanded. It cannot be imposed. It is not built on fear. A child who feels free to leave will return with warmth, respect, and love. A child who feels they *must* stay will carry resentment. The parent-child relationship should not be a transaction, but a space of freedom, trust, and mutual respect. And let us not forget love.

The fear of loneliness is real. At times, it is painful. But it should not be treated with solutions that involve other lives. It requires introspection, healing, and the building of authentic relationships —not the creation of obligations. Having a child should not be an emotional survival strategy, but a choice born from mature love, not from fear.

There is a subtle form of loneliness that creeps into the soul even when surrounded by people. It is that feeling that no one truly perceives you, that your presence goes unnoticed, like an echo in a crowded room. And here lies the paradox: I want others to see, respect, and appreciate me, but how can they do that if I do not appreciate myself?

In the attempt to build self-confidence—to zoom in on what is going well in a person's life and identify the "toolkit" they carry toward their therapeutic goals—I often ask my clients: "Who are you? What are your strengths?" It often takes a long time to get an answer to this simple question. Sometimes 10–15 minutes pass before we can identify just three or four traits. And yet, we crave appreciation from others. How can that happen if we do not see ourselves?

Psychologically, this state occurs when the need for emotional connection is not met, and the individual feels disconnected from others even if social interaction continues. It is a rupture between what is visible on the surface and what is felt deep down—a discrepancy between appearance and authenticity. In such moments, loneliness is not about the absence of others, but about the absence of a space where you can be yourself, without a mask, without fear.

A child is not a crutch or a bandage. They are not a guarantee. They are a being who deserves to be wanted for who they are, not for what they can do.

Unfortunately, many parents resort to emotional blackmail as a form of control, often masked as love or moral duty. Expressions like "I made you, I can break you" (or "I brought you into this world, and I can take you out") or "After all the sacrifices I made for you..." are not just painful; they are deeply destructive. They transform the parent-child relationship into a conditional contract based on guilt and obligation, rather than authentic affection.

Regarding the idea that "it is the child's duty to care for the parents, just as they cared for him," it must be stated clearly: physically, emotionally, and psychologically, this is impossible. A child cannot replicate exactly what they received for the simple reason that the power balance, vulnerability, and responsibility are fundamentally different. A parent's role is that of a protector, guide, and support in forming the child's identity. Reversing this role cannot be symmetrical because a formed adult no longer has the same needs as a developing child.

Furthermore, the idea of "duty" in affective relationships is dangerous. It replaces freedom with obligation and love with moral pressure. Care for parents should stem from gratitude and affection, not from fear or guilt. When a parent demands back what they have given, they turn the act of love into a currency of exchange, canceling its very essence.

There is an old proverb: "You reap what you sow." I mentioned this for a reason. There are parents who brought at least one child into the world for various reasons, yet raised them in a toxic, unsuitable environment—one where love, presence, encouragement, and positive role models were absent. Moreover, there was humiliation, neglect, and physical and emotional abuse. And yet, these parents expect, when the time comes, to be cared for and loved by their children. The power of example is astonishing. If they receive indifference and neglect—just as they likely gave—those same parents are dissatisfied. They project this general dissatisfaction as guilt onto their children—a guilt that, in some cases, requires years of psychotherapy to heal.

It is a painful reversal of responsibility: the parent who did not offer love demands, at maturity, unconditional love, as if the child were duty-bound to repair what they themselves never received.

3.1. Implications and Consequences

A parent-child relationship born out of the fear of loneliness does not stem from a place of abundance, but from a void. And this void, no matter how well masked, seeps into gestures, words, and silences. It becomes an invisible presence that shapes everything. Similarly, the motivation to have a child solely to secure one's old age does not create a free, fruitful relationship. For the parent, the child becomes a sort of emotional guarantee—not just a beloved being, but an anchor in an uncertain future. This projection creates a relationship where love is accompanied by fear: the fear of being forgotten, of being abandoned, of not being enough. In moments of vulnerability, the parent may experience negative thoughts: "I did everything for them, and now I'm being ignored," "I don't deserve to be alone," "Other people's children are more grateful."

As mentioned, the parent feels a chronic fear of abandonment; this can be the central theme for many. Even when the child is small, when they are present and saying "I love you," the parent feels an underlying anxiety: "Will they stay by my side?" "Will they still love me when they grow up?" "What will happen if I get sick?" Even if these thoughts are not explicitly communicated to the child, they take the place of other messages that carry guilt and accusations: "You'll surely leave me when you're grown," "You'll forget about me after all the sacrifices I've made for you."

These thoughts do not remain isolated. They transform into negative emotions: resentment, sadness, shame, and repressed anger. The parent may become passive-aggressive, manipulative, or excessively dependent. The relationship becomes burdened with subtle tensions and conflicts.

This fear of abandonment transforms into emotional control. The parent does not ask explicitly, but they expect. They do not impose, but they suggest. They do not reproach directly, but they withdraw, become saddened, or play the victim. The child quickly learns that the parent's emotional state depends on them. And this becomes an unfair emotional responsibility.

In time, the parent can become a prisoner of their own projections. They imagine a future where the child will be there will provide care, will be a support. Consequently, any sign of independence from the child is perceived as a threat.

For the child, this dynamic is like a body of water they learn to swim in, without realizing it is murky and swampy. They feel they must be "good," "present," and "grateful." Not because it is explicitly demanded, but because the absence of these things seems to cause pain. Thus, the child learns to self-erase: they suppress their desires, censor their needs, and build an identity based on what is "expected" of them.

The child senses early on that love is conditional. It isn't said directly, but they feel it: in the moments the parent becomes saddened when the child wants to leave, or when they are praised for obedience but criticized for autonomy.

They grow up with a diffuse sense of guilt: "I have to be there," "I can't hurt them," "If I leave, I'll destroy them." Guilt becomes part of their identity. They define themselves by what they offer, not by who they are.

This latent guilt becomes a "red thread" throughout their life. They feel responsible for the parent's emotional state, and in their adult relationships, they repeat the same pattern: they become the "rescuer," they sacrifice themselves, and they lose themselves in the needs of others. Or, at the other extreme, they isolate themselves, refusing any form of attachment for fear of being "used" as a support again.

Inside them, a battle rages between the desire for freedom and the need not to cause pain—between who they want to be and who they feel they must be. This struggle exhausts them, makes them fragile, and causes them to doubt their own choices.

A strained dynamic settles into the parent-child relationship: love is present, but it is accompanied by conditions. Communication becomes fragmented, filled with heavy silences, gestures that speak louder than words, and veiled reproaches that hurt more than direct ones.

In moments of crisis, the relationship can explode: the child rebels and the parent feels betrayed. Or, more often, the relationship slowly fades into an affective routine where love is present, but accompanied by emotional exhaustion, frustration, and unspoken misunderstandings.

Over time, the relationship can become choreography of need and guilt. Each plays their role, but no one feels truly free, loved, or appreciated. And freedom, in this context, seems like a luxury that no one can afford.

3.2. Alternatives and Reflections

Having a child out of the fear of loneliness or as a means of support in old age is a choice that may seem justifiable, but it carries profound emotional risks. If the motivation is not authentic, the parent-child relationship risks becoming conditional, strained, and fragile.

Before deciding to become parents, those facing the fear of loneliness or anxiety regarding old age can identify alternatives that better suit their needs:

- **I can work through fears in a psychotherapeutic context.** Fears do not disappear if they are ignored; instead, they transform into shadows that follow us into our relationships, decisions, and gestures.
- **Accepting solitude as a part of life.** Solitude can be viewed not as a punishment, but as an opportunity. It teaches us to listen to ourselves, to contain our emotions, and to discover who we are. It is a space where we can become whole and explore our true potential.
- **Reframing old age.** This stage of life, though natural, is often associated with fragility, isolation, or helplessness. However, it can also be seen as a period of creativity, mentorship, freedom, and reinvention—a time of liberation from social pressures, where one can finally turn inward. One can create, not for validation, but for pure joy; one can share, not out of obligation, but out of generosity.
- **Repairing the parent-child relationship.** Yes, this relationship can be mended—not perfectly, but with sincerity. This happens through dialogue, by respecting the path the child has chosen, and through small gestures that prove love.
- **Expanding social networks and passions.** When your life rests on a single pillar—namely, your relationship with your child—and that child grows into an independent adult, it becomes difficult to find meaning again. Build social connections and engage in activities that are meaningful to you (volunteering, personal projects, discovering new hobbies, senior clubs, etc.).

Reflection Questions

- Which part of me fears loneliness? What do I need to heal within that space?
- Do I want a child for who they are, or for what they can do for me?
- What does old age mean to me? What scares me about it, and what can I build within that stage of life?
- How can I create relationships where affection is given freely, not conditionally?
- What can I do today to become more emotionally autonomous?
- What would I say to my child if I could be completely honest? What would I want to hear from them?

Chapter 4

Unhealthy Motivation 2: The Child as a Replacement

„Unprocessed pain is passed on. A child inherits not only genes, but also the silences, the fears, and the unspoken desires of their parents."

Françoise Dolto

This chapter explores a deeply unhealthy motivation that can emerge following a devastating loss: the death of a child or a pregnancy loss. Faced with such trauma, a parent may remain stuck in unprocessed grief, and the arrival of a new child becomes, without conscious intent, an attempt at replacement. This is not about forgetting; it is about emotional survival.

The loss of a child or a pregnancy is one of the most shattering experiences a parent can endure. In the face of such pain, some people choose to bring another child into the world, not necessarily out of a desire for a new family member, but out of a need to fill a void. This motivation is born from trauma—from a desire to repair, to heal, and to rewrite a story that ended too soon.

There are pains that are not expressed, but embodied. They hide in gestures, in choices, and in silences. The death of a child leaves behind a rupture that does not close with time, but through integration. And when this integration does not take place, the pain transforms. It shifts. It reconfigures itself within the relationship with the child who comes "after."

This child is not just a new beginning. They are, without the parent fully realizing it, an attempt at reparation—a bridge between what was and what could no longer be. They are invested with an impossible task: to soothe, to compensate, to revive, and to replace. They are not allowed to simply be themselves. They are viewed through the lens of loss, and the love offered to them carries an inherent tension: between presence and absence, between hope and fear.

The parent does not do this out of a lack of love, but out of an inability to process a trauma that has torn their identity apart. Instead of grieving, they build. Instead of accepting, they project. The child who comes after such a loss becomes a symbol, a function, a mission. Consequently, the relationship becomes burdened with unspoken expectations, intense anxieties, and subtle comparisons. There is a desire for them to be "healthier," "better," "closer." Every risk, every distancing, and every bit of autonomy is avoided, because loss can no longer be tolerated a second time.

But the child senses it. They sense they are not loved solely for who they are, but for who they were supposed to be. They feel that their freedom comes at a cost: the parent's pain. And they learn to conform, to sacrifice themselves, and to hide. Or, on the contrary, they rebel, they break away, and they distance themselves—filled with guilt, anger, and confusion.

This dynamic is not easy to recognize, for it hides under the guise of care, protection, and involvement. But at its core, it is a form of self-avoidance. A flight from mourning. An inability to say: "I have lost. And I must moan."

Furthermore, this dynamic is rarely discussed, precisely because it masks itself as love. But at its core, it is a confusion between presence and absence—between who the child is and who they were "supposed" to be.

There are gestures that seem natural on the surface but carry a silent, often unexplored symbolic weight. Choosing to give a child born after a loss the name of their deceased sibling is one of them. Outwardly, it is a tribute, a form of continuity, an attempt to keep a memory alive. But deeply, it is an identity imprinting that can influence the child's destiny in a subtle yet persistent way.

The child who carries the name of a lost sibling is no longer just themselves. They unintentionally become the bearer of a memory, a pain, and an unfulfilled hope. A name is not just a label; it is a calling, a comparison, a projection of a lost ideal. In the parent's mind, even if left unsaid, thoughts may emerge such as: *"The first one would have been better," "They wouldn't have done that," "This one isn't as obedient."* And the child senses it. They feel they are living in a shadow. That they must compensate. That they are not enough. That they do not belong. They feel that the love they receive is not entirely free, but entangled with a desire for reparation.

This dynamic can lead to identity confusion, latent guilt, and difficulties in self-assertion. The child may become excessively obedient in an attempt to avoid disappointing the parent. Or, conversely, they may rebel, feeling they have no space to be who they truly are. In either case, they live with an inner tension:

between the desire to be loved and the need to detach from an identity that does not belong to them.

For the parent, this choice may seem like an act of love. But if it is not accompanied by the conscious processing of grief, it becomes a form of avoidance—an attempt to keep alive what is no longer there through what is just beginning. Thus, the beginning is contaminated by the past.

A child born after trauma must not be a replica. They do not need to be better, more obedient, or more "correct." They need to be themselves. True love begins where the parent can say: *"I see you. Not as someone who was, but as someone who is."*

Sometimes, the parent does not realize they are living in the past. The lost child's room remains unchanged, their name is spoken frequently, or, on the contrary, never mentioned at all, and the new child grows up in the shadow of an absence that becomes omnipresent. The untouched room, hidden photographs, or the secrecy surrounding the death are evidence that the loss has not been processed.

To understand this dynamic, it is essential to look through the lens of the five stages of grief, as formulated by Elisabeth Kübler-Ross:

- **Denial and Shock:** In the beginning, the parent may refuse to accept the loss. They might continue to speak about the deceased child as if they were still present. At this stage, a child born afterward may be perceived as a natural "continuation" rather than a distinct being.
- **Anger:** Pain transforms into revolt. The parent may feel anger toward doctors, toward themselves, or toward fate.

Sometimes, this anger is unconsciously projected onto the newborn child, who is seen as "not the same," "not enough," or "not the one who was supposed to be here."

- **Bargaining:** The mind tries to find meaning. Thoughts emerge such as: *"If this child is obedient, perhaps the pain will diminish."* The child is invested with unrealistic expectations, as if they could "redeem" or make up for the loss.
- **Depression:** The reality of the loss sets in. The parent may become distant, overwhelmed, and emotionally absent. The child senses this absence but cannot understand it. They may feel rejected, unimportant, or inadequate.
- **Acceptance:** This is the stage where the parent begins to integrate the pain. They do not forget it, but they acknowledge it. In this stage, the child can finally be seen for who they truly are—not as a replacement, but as a unique being with their own path.

Processed grief does not mean forgetting, nor does it mean the cancellation of loss. It does not mean closing your eyes and moving on as if nothing had happened. Authentic grief is a journey—sometimes slow, painful, and contradictory—through every layer of suffering. It is an ownership of absence, an acknowledgment of the rupture, and an integration of what can no longer be changed.

To process grief means to allow the pain to exist without turning it into a burden for someone else. It means honoring the life that has ended without projecting it onto the one that is just beginning. Ultimately, it is an act of mature love: to be able to say, "I lost you," without asking someone else to fix you.

The very act of phrasing it in simple words, such as "my first child died," is part of acceptance. Most of the time, people refer to death using other formulations: "they left," "since they are no longer here," "they disappeared," "they passed away," "they went to the other side," and so on.

4.1. Implications and Consequences

When a child is brought into the world following the loss of the first, without the grief having been processed, the entire parent-child relationship is built on fragile, often unstable ground. The new child can unintentionally become an emotional substitute —an attempt to repair a wound that is impossible to heal through another life. This dynamic generates profound implications for both parent and child.

For the parent, two extreme tendencies may emerge: overprotectiveness—a constant fear of losing again, leading to excessive control, anxiety, and the limitation of the child's autonomy; or, conversely, emotional detachment—an avoidance of attachment, born from the unconscious conviction that closeness brings suffering: "If I lose them, it's better not to get attached." Both reactions deeply affect the emotional development of the child, who feels either suffocated or subtly abandoned. Furthermore, this affects the parent's emotional balance as well, as they live in a state of continuous fear and hypervigilance.

In cases where the lost child was of a different sex than the child born afterward, gender projections may occur: a girl might be pushed toward masculine activities or roles that belonged to the lost brother. Thus, the child's identity is shaped not by who they are, but by who the other was. The child grows up with a subtle confusion: "Who am I, really?"

Another essential aspect is the secret. In many families, the death of the previous child is hidden, unspoken, and unaddressed. The child senses a tension, a heavy silence, but does not understand its source. This secret becomes an invisible burden: it generates guilt, shame, and pressure, all without a clear explanation. The child may feel they must be "perfect," never to disappoint or cause suffering. In the absence of the truth, they construct their own explanations—often painful and distorted. Sometimes it is easy to tell when a secret exists: when sensitive topics are touched upon, the conversation is abruptly diverted without explanation; the parents' faces change instantly; one parent stands up and leaves, unable to bear the continuation of the discussion; or there are places in the house where one is not allowed to go.

One of the most painful consequences is the sense of non-belonging. The child may feel they have no real place in the family—that they were not wanted for who they are, but for what they were meant to replace. This perception of being "extra" or unworthy of unconditional love can become a profound identity wound. it may manifest as withdrawal, anxiety, difficulties in relationships, or even self-rejection.

The consequences extend into future relationships—into the way the child relates to love, to loss, and to themselves. They may become hyper-responsible, anxious, and plagued by an acute need for validation. Or, conversely, they may reject any form of closeness, fearing they will again be "replaced" or that they will cause pain.

For the parent, failing to process grief means that the relationship with the new child is always overshadowed by the past. It is not an authentic encounter, but a reenactment. Only by taking ownership of the loss, acknowledging the pain, and releasing the child from the role of "replacement" can a healthy relationship be built—one based on presence, not absence.

I remember a 45-year-old client who shared during therapy: "I am the oldest of the children; I have a younger brother. At the age of 20, I found out by mistake that my parents had lost their first child at six months old. To this day, I don't know why. My mother died without ever telling me, and my father won't speak about it. Until I was 20, I felt like an intruder in my own family; I had no place, and I felt as though I was suffocating."

4.2 Alternatives and Reflections

Having a child after the loss of another may seem like a natural way to move forward. However, if this choice is made out of a need to fill a void, to repair a trauma, or to replace an absence, the relationship with the new child risks being burdened by projections, tensions, and misunderstandings. A child cannot heal a wound that the parent has not had the courage to face directly.

Before deciding to become parents again, those who have experienced the loss of a child can explore alternatives that offer space for healing and reconstruction:

Processing grief within a therapeutic framework. Unfaced pain does not disappear; instead, it transforms into heavy silences, diffuse fears, and disproportionate reactions. Speaking about the loss, understanding it, and giving it a place within one's personal story is an act of liberation.

Separating identities. The new child is not a continuation, a replica, or a function. They are a unique being with their own path. Seeing them for who they are, rather than for who is missing, means granting them the freedom to *be*.

Building a relationship based on presence, not compensation. Being there, day by day, without demanding perfection, without projecting fear, and without conditioning love. Learning to love again, not as an escape from pain, but as a conscious choice.

Integrating the lost child into affective memory. Speaking about them, preserving their memory, and acknowledging their place can release the invisible tension weighing upon the child born afterward. Secrecy does not protect. The truth, told with gentleness, can become a space for reconnection.

Reconstructing personal meaning. Being a parent should not be the sole source of identity. Cultivating passions, social relationships, and personal projects can bring balance and purpose. Healing does not come only from the outside, but also from the capacity to find oneself again.

Reflection Questions

- What part of me remains unhealed after the loss?
- Do I want a child for who they are, or because someone else is no longer here?
- What expectations do I hold for my child that I have never voiced?
- How can I honor the memory of the lost child without projecting it onto the one present now?

- What can I do today to build an authentic relationship, rather than a compensatory one?
- What would I say to my child if I could be completely honest? What would I want to hear from them?

Chapter 5

Unhealthy Motivation 3: The Child as a Playmate

„Children are like wet cement.
Whatever falls on them makes an impression."
Dr. Haim Ginott

There are moments in a parent's life when the desire to have another child is not born out of an authentic need to expand the family, but out of a projection onto the existing child. 'So they won't be alone,' 'To have someone to play with,' 'To keep them from being selfish' – these are phrases that seem innocent, but they can hide a deeply unhealthy motivation: the new child is not wanted for who they are, but for what they can offer the other.

This choice—to bring a child into the world as a playmate for their brother or sister—may seem simple and friendly. But, at its core, it transforms the child into a function. They are not seen as a unique being, but as an extension, a relational accessory meant to complete, balance, or entertain. They are not desired for their own sake, but for the role they are expected to play.

In such contexts, the parent may project a series of unrealistic expectations onto the sibling relationship: that they always be together, get along perfectly, never fight, and protect each other. Any conflict between them becomes a source of disappointment, proof that the 'plan' didn't work. And the child brought into the world with this motivation feels the pressure. They feel they must be 'good,' 'gentle,' and 'compatible.' They feel they aren't allowed to withdraw, to assert themselves, or to differentiate.

Sometimes, the desire to have 'two children close in age' does not stem from an authentic need for love, but from a subtle fear: the fear that the first child will be lonely, will become 'too selfish,' or will suffer from the lack of a constant presence. In reality, this fear does not belong to the child, but to the parent. It is a projection, anticipation, an avoidance of one's own loneliness, disguised as care. Of course, there is also the fear that, over time, patience erodes and, if they wait too long, the parents in question will be left with an only child. Here, the 'biological clock' might also intervene—after all, 'I'm not going to have a child at 40 or 45.'

This dynamic can manifest in seemingly natural gestures: choosing to buy them the same clothes, giving them the same toys, or enrolling them in the same activities. Differences are avoided; symbiosis is promoted. But do parents truly not differentiate between their children? And when one of the children begins to detach, to assert their preferences, the parent may feel a sense of rupture—as if the desired harmony is falling apart.

But harmony is not built through uniformity. It is built through recognition, through the acceptance of differences and the validation of individuality. Children are not extensions of one another. They are not puzzle pieces that must fit together perfectly. They are distinct worlds, with their own rhythms, different needs, and separate paths.

For the child brought into the world with this motivation, the pressure can be overwhelming. They feel they must be 'good,' 'gentle,' and 'compatible.' They feel they are not allowed to withdraw, to assert themselves, or to differentiate. And if they do, they feel guilty—as if they are betraying the very purpose for which they were wanted.

In some cases, the sibling relationship becomes symbiotic, but not healthy. An emotional dependency develops a fear of separation, and a difficulty in asserting the self. In other cases, rivalry emerges: the child feels they cannot be themselves that they must conform, that they have no room to breathe. And this tension turns into conflict, withdrawal, or rebellion.

For the parent, acknowledging this motivation is painful. It involves a confrontation with their own unexpressed needs: the fear of loneliness, the desire for control, and the idealization of the sibling relationship. Yet, it is also an opportunity—to truly see the child. To build a relationship based on presence, not on projection. To learn that love does not mean symbiosis, but freedom.

A child should not be a predestined playmate. They do not have to be 'compatible,' 'complementary,' or 'ideal.' They need to be themselves. And true love begins where the parent can say: 'I see you. Not for what you bring to the other, but for who you are.'

Sometimes, the child who arrives 'for the sake of the other' is not just a playmate, but also a guardian of the parent's loneliness. They are expected to fill empty spaces, to bring harmony, to repair tensions. But a child cannot be their sibling's therapist, or their parents' mediator, or the guarantor of someone else's happy childhood. They need to be seen for themselves, not for the role they play in the family equilibrium.

In many families, this dynamic is unconscious. People speak of 'balance,' the 'beauty of being two,' or 'mutual support.' But beneath these ideals, avoidance may be hidden: the avoidance of confronting each child's real needs. It is assumed that if they are together, they will be fine. That if they play, they love each other. That if they don't fight, the parent has succeeded.

But children are not guarantors of parental success. They are beings in the making, with different rhythms, contradictory needs, and desires that do not always align. And when one of them feels they aren't allowed to be different, to detach, or to assert themselves, a rupture occurs—not always between the siblings, but between the child and their own self, or between the parent and the child.

There are children who grow up feeling they cannot be alone—that they must always be 'with someone,' must conform, must adapt. This is because they were raised with the idea that their existence is valuable only in relation to another. They haven't learned to be by themselves, to listen to their own voice, or to choose themselves. Later in life, this lack of autonomy can turn into mutually supporting relationships, fear of separation, and difficulties with self-assertion.

For the parent who chose to bring a child into the world as a playmate, healing begins with a simple, perhaps difficult question: 'Did I want them for who they are, or for what they could provide for the other?' This is a question that does not accuse, but liberates. Because within that honest answer lies the beginning of an authentic relationship.

A child should not be a gift for their sibling. They should not be a solution, a completion, or a function. They must be a whole being, with the right to be different, to detach, and to assert them. True love begins when the parent can say: 'I didn't bring you here for anyone else. I brought you here for you.'

5.1. Implications and Consequences

When a child is brought into the world with the motivation of being a playmate for their brother or sister, the entire relational construct is based on a function, not an identity. The child is not desired for who they are, but for what they can provide for the other. This projection though masked as care and good intentions can have profound consequences on the emotional and relational development of both children.

For the child "brought for the other," a subtle sense of illegitimacy may take root. They feel they have no place of their own, that they are not enough in themselves, and that their existence is justified only in relation to the older sibling. This perception can generate identity confusion: "Who am I, if I am not what is expected of me?" Over time, the child may become hyper-adaptive, avoiding conflict, repressing their own desires, and living under a silent pressure to be "compatible."

In some cases, an emotional dependency develops between siblings where autonomy is sacrificed in favor of symbiosis. The child does not learn to be alone, to listen to themselves, or to choose themselves. In other cases, the relationship turns into rivalry: the child feels they must compete for attention, validation, and space. Without realizing it, the parent may fuel this tension through subtle comparisons, unspoken expectations, or by idealizing the sibling bond.

The parent who has projected this motivation may experience contradictory reactions. On one hand, there is disappointment when the children do not get along "as they should." On the other hand, there is difficulty in seeing each child as a distinct being with their own needs and rhythms. The parent may become excessively involved in the sibling dynamics, neglecting the individual relationship with each child. Yes, time spent together is necessary, but so is separate, one-on-one time with each child.

This unhealthy motivation can also affect the parent's emotional balance, leading to continuous tension: the desire for harmony, the fear of conflict, and the need for validation through the "success" of the children's relationship. When reality fails to meet the ideal, frustration, guilt, and withdrawal emerge.

In therapy, I met a mother who said: "I had the second child so the first wouldn't be alone. But now they fight all the time and I feel I've made a mistake. My eldest daughter tells me she feels like a nanny to her sister, while the younger one is always invading her personal space, constantly looking to play. There is a four-year gap between them. Even though we always buy them the exact same toys so they won't argue, the conflicts still happen." Hidden behind this statement was a profound pain: her own need to avoid loneliness, to create a "perfect" family, and to repair a childhood in which she herself had been lonely. The child had not been wanted for who she was, but for what she could bring to the family equation.

Each of the two girls has a role: one of supervision and attention, the other of providing the playfulness. At the ages of 3 and 7, their toy preferences and cognitive needs are different; yet, the parents want to bring them to a common denominator. Implicitly, the eldest daughter is "allowed" to stagnate.

For the child, this dynamic can leave deep scars: difficulties in friendships, fear of separation, the need to always be a "people pleaser," and an inability to assert oneself. In future relationships, they may become emotionally dependent, anxious, or, conversely, distant and distrustful. This is because they never learned that they have value in themselves, but only in relation to someone else.

Only by recognizing this motivation, processing one's real needs, and releasing the child from the role of "playmate" can the parent build an authentic relationship—one where the child is seen, heard, and respected, not for what they offer the other, but for who they truly are.

5.2. Alternatives and Reflections

Having a child just so the existing one 'won't be alone' may seem like a natural, even generous choice. However, if this decision is motivated by a fear of isolation, social pressure, or the ideal of a 'complete' family, the relationship with the new child risks being built on unspoken expectations, imposed roles, and unprocessed needs. A child cannot fill a void that the parent has not understood. They cannot be the guarantor of a harmonious sibling relationship. They cannot be responsible for the other's happiness.

Before deciding to bring a new child into the family, parents can explore alternatives that offer space for clarity, authenticity, and conscious choice:

- Exploring the real motivation within a therapeutic setting. The desire to avoid loneliness, to create an ideal family image, or to heal one's own childhood wounds can influence parental decisions. Understanding, naming, and processing these needs is an act of emotional responsibility.

- Separating relationships. Every child deserves to be seen as a unique being, not as an extension of their brother or sister. Welcoming them for who they are, rather than for what they can provide to another, means respecting their identity and allowing them to develop freely.
- Building a relationship based on choice, not function. Being there for the child every day without conditioning them to be the "perfect friend" or "ideal companion." Loving them for who they are, not for the role they play in the family dynamics.
- Cultivating the sibling relationship without pressure. Creating contexts for closeness while also respecting differences. Encouraging empathy as well as autonomy. Accepting that children sometimes do not get along and that this is not a failure, but a natural part of human relationships.
- Reconnecting with oneself as a parent. Being a parent does not only mean building relationships between children, but also building authentic relationships with each of them. Asking yourself what kind of parent you want to be, what values you want to transmit, and what emotional space you offer.
- Discussing, communicating, and negotiating important decisions with one's partner. Bringing a new child into the family is a choice that involves both parents, not just in terms of responsibility, but as an affective process. Speaking openly about desires, fears, projections, and needs can prevent future tensions and strengthen the couple's relationship. The child is

not an individual project, but an extension of a relationship that deserves to be clear, honest, and conscious.

Reflection Questions

- What part of me fears loneliness and projects it onto the child?
- Do I want a child for who they are, or for what I believe they will bring to the other?
- What roles am I imposing on my children without realizing it?
- How can I cultivate authentic relationships between siblings without forcing their compatibility?
- What can I do today to see each child as a unique being, rather than a part of a system?

Chapter 6

Unhealthy Motivation 4: The Child as a Lifesaver

„A child cannot be the salvation of the parents. If they are invested with this mission, they will carry a burden that does not belong to them."

Bert Hellinger

Sometimes, in the darkest corners of despair, a hope is born that wears the face of a child. Not from the desire to love, but from the need to save. Not from the dream of a family, but from the fear of loss. There are rare, yet not non-existent, situations where a child comes into the world with a mission already mapped out: to heal, to repair, to prolong someone else's life. It may be a sick sibling, a mother on the brink of death, or a father clinging to a last chance. And the child becomes, without knowing, without choosing, an instrument of salvation.

Sometimes, a child is conceived to be genetically compatible with a sick sibling when other family members cannot be donors. This involves bone marrow transplants, stem cells, or even organs in extreme situations. In such contexts, parents are in a race against time, and the decision to bring a new child into the world becomes a desperate choice between life and death.

A frequent example is that of children born to donate stem cells to siblings suffering from leukemia. Genetic compatibility is essential, and the chances of a sibling being a suitable donor are limited. If the parents are not compatible and the donor bank offers no solutions, conceiving a child becomes, in their minds, the only way. In other cases, a child is brought into the world to donate an organ (a kidney, for example) when a parent or sibling is in severe renal failure. Although such interventions are rare and strictly regulated, the intention behind them remains the same: saving a life through a new life.

There are also less visible, but equally emotionally charged situations, where a child is born with the hope that they will bring balance to a family adrift. A mother suffering from severe depression may believe that a new child will give her meaning, a motivation to live. A father who has lost a previous child may hope that a newborn will fill a void. In these cases, the child is not meant to save through blood or organs, but through presence—to heal a wound, to repair a trauma, to bring light into a devastated inner space.

But what happens when the child grows up and begins to feel, even without being told directly, that their existence is tied to a mission? That the love they receive is accompanied by a silent expectation? That their freedom to be who they are clashes with the need to be the "savior"? In such cases, the child's identity may be built on a fragile foundation, where personal value is confused with utility. And this can lead to profound inner conflicts, to guilt, and to the need to constantly prove themselves "worthy" of the love they receive.

It is essential to understand that a child should never be the answer to a problem, no matter how serious it may be. They deserve to be wanted for who they are, not for what they can save. They deserve to be loved without conditions, not because they can rescue, heal, or repair. Parents who find themselves in such situations need support, counseling, and space to process their pain—before making a decision that will mark not only their lives but also the life of a being who had no say in the matter.

In such contexts, the boundary between love and obligation becomes blurred. The parent, overwhelmed by grief, may project disproportionate expectations onto the child, and the child, in an attempt to be "enough," may end up losing themselves. It is a fragile dynamic that requires a great deal of awareness and healing. Because no child should carry the burden of saving a life on their shoulders. They deserve to be loved for who they are, not for what they can do.

Bringing a child into the world is, in essence, an act of creation, of love, of opening oneself to the unknown. But when this decision is rooted in a need for salvation, it risks becoming a projection of pain rather than a celebration of life. A child is not an antidote, they are not a bandage, they are not a solution. They are a whole being, with the right to be wanted, not necessary. With the right to be loved, not utilized. With the right to be free, not conditioned.

It takes great courage for a parent to acknowledge their own suffering and to separate it from the desire to have a child. Healing is needed before creation. Otherwise, the child will carry a story that does not belong to them, a mission they did not choose, a burden that may break their wings before they learn to fly.

And perhaps it is precisely in this awareness that the beginning of an authentic relationship lies. One where the child is not the savior, but simply the child. Loved for who they are, not for what they can do. Viewed with gratitude, not with expectation. Raised with freedom, not with pressure. Because only then will their life truly be their own.

If you feel this ending is appropriate, we can move on to choosing a quote to close the chapter with power and resonance. Would you like me to propose a few options, or do you already have one in mind?

6.1. Implications and Consequences

The implications of such a motivation branch deep into the family's emotional structure. They are not immediately visible, nor do they manifest loudly; instead, they seep into relationships, identities, and silences. Each member involved carries a different story, a different burden, a different wound.

For the parent, the decision to bring a child into the world for the purpose of saving someone else is, in essence, a choice made out of love, but also out of despair. It is a form of sacrifice that may seem noble, yet hides a profound tension. The parent may live with a latent guilt, with unspoken questions: "Did I do the right thing?", "Did I truly want this child, or did I just use him?", "Do I love him for who he is, or for what he has done?". These questions may remain unvoiced, but they shape the relationship, weighing it down and making it fragile. The parent may fluctuate between gratitude and shame, between love and doubt.

For the "savior" child, existence becomes a mission. Even if no one tells them directly, they feel it. They feel it in the glances, in the gestures, in the way they are treated. They may feel they must be "good," "responsible," "worthy" of their role—that they are not allowed to make mistakes, to disappoint, or to stray from the path laid out for them. This often-invisible pressure can lead to anxiety, a loss of identity, and a constant need for validation. The child may become the adult who always feels insufficient, always searching for meaning, always struggling to deserve love.

For the saved child or family member, the relationship with the savior sibling can be fraught with guilt. They may feel that their existence was "bought" with someone else's life. That they must be grateful, that they have no right to complain, and that they must live "beautifully" to justify the sacrifice. This guilt can erode the relationship, create distance, and transform love into an obligation. In some cases, the saved child may feel unworthy of the effort made for them, a feeling that can lead to depression, withdrawal, and internal fractures that are difficult to heal.

In this context, the parent-child relationship becomes a complicated equation. The parent may project disproportionate expectations onto the child, and the child may feel that the love they receive is conditional. A dynamic can emerge where freedom is replaced by obligation, and authenticity is sacrificed in favor of an imposed role. Love exists, but it is accompanied by a subtle tension, an untold story, and a pain that has no words.

For the entire family, this decision can become a core around which all relationships gravitate. It can create alliances, resentments, and silences. It can bring closeness, but also fractures. It can transform the family into a space where everyone wears a mask, plays a role, and carries a story that does not truly belong to them. And healing, if it comes, requires a great deal of awareness, honesty, and courage.

Because, ultimately, every child deserves to be wanted for whom he is. Not for what they can save. Because his life has value in itself. Because true love asks for nothing in return.

6.2. Alternatives and Reflections

Bringing a child into the world to save the life of another may seem, in moments of crisis, like the only option. It is a choice born out of love, but also out of fear—out of a desire to preserve, to repair, and to not let go. However, if this decision is not accompanied by a profound processing of grief and an awareness of its implications, the child risks being entrusted with a mission that does not belong to them. Consequently, the relationship with them can become an equation of expectations, rather than a space of freedom.

There are alternatives that do not erase the pain, but can transform it—alternatives that do not offer magic solutions, but can open paths that are more authentic, more free, and more human:

· Processing trauma within a therapeutic framework. Before making a decision that will mark a lifetime, a parent needs to understand their own suffering—to name it, to feel it, and to move through it. Unprocessed pain does not disappear; it transforms into projections, tensions, and burdened relationships. Speaking about loss, fear, and powerlessness is an act of emotional maturity.

- Separating the need for rescue from the desire to be a parent. Being a parent is not about fixing, but about accompanying.

It is not about demanding, but about offering. It is not about projecting, but about seeing. A child should not be an answer to a problem, but a being wanted for who they are, not for what they can do.

- Building a relationship based on presence, not on a mission. To be there, day by day, without demanding performance, without conditioning love, and without turning the child's existence into an act of compensation. To love them for whom they are, not for what they bring. To look at them with clear eyes, not with burdened hopes.
- Discussing major decisions with one's partner. A choice of such intensity cannot be unilateral. It is essential for both parents to express their fears, desires, and projections—to listen to, confront, and understand one another. A child is not an individual project, but an extension of a relationship that deserves to be clear, sincere, and conscious.
- Exploring other forms of healing. Sometimes, salvation does not come from the outside, but from within—from the capacity to accept, to understand, and to transform pain into meaning. Cultivating relationships, passions, and personal projects can bring balance. Life is not rebuilt through a new start, but through the integration of what has been.

Reflection Questions

- What part of me has not yet been healed and is seeking salvation through a child?
- Do I want a child for who they are, or for what I hope they will repair?

- What expectations do I carry within me that have remained unspoken?
- How can I build a relationship based on freedom, rather than obligation?
- What can I do today to transform pain into meaning, instead of a mission?
- How can I take ownership of my pain without turning it into a mission for someone else?
- What other forms of meaning can I build without placing this responsibility on the shoulders of a being that did not choose it?

Chapter 7

Unhealthy Motivation 5: The Child as a Second Chance for the Parent's Lost Childhood

---

„A child is not a second chance. He is a first chance—his own."

Cristina Nica

There is a subtle form of love that, while appearing generous, hides a deep wound: the desire for one's own child to live what the parent was not allowed, was unable, or did not know how to live. It is a love that is not offered freely, but is projected. The child is not seen as a separate being, but as an extension of the wounded self. A second chance. A repair.

This motivation often arises following a childhood lived in absence—the absence of freedom, validation, or authentic joy. The parent who was not heard, who was not allowed to make mistakes, which was not encouraged to dream, transforms their child into a symbol of hope. "My child will have everything I lacked." But within this promise, made by the parent to themselves, lies a trap: the child is not allowed to be themselves, but is instead pushed to become what the parent could not.

On the surface, everything seems generous. The parent provides, protects, and invests. They dedicate their time, resources, and energy, building their life around the child. But deep down, the child is conditioned to perform, to fulfill, and to not disappoint. They are not asked for authenticity, but for excellence. They are not offered freedom, but a mission. A burden.

The child feels the pressure, even if they do not understand it. They feel they must be "something," become "someone," and never fail. But they do not know why. They do not know they are carrying a story that is not theirs. And so, they begin to lose themselves. To doubt. To ask: "Who am I, beyond what is expected of me?"

Let us pause here for a moment: "My child will have everything I lacked!" This is a promise spoken perhaps with tears in one's eyes, with trembling hands and a heart full of longing. It is a phrase that seems to express supreme love, but in reality, it hides a silent struggle, a massive pressure, and confusion between the need to give and the need to heal. But what, and whom, are you healing?

For some parents, this promise becomes a life project. It transforms into financial efforts that far exceed their actual means. They work overtime, sacrifice their health, and ignore their limits—all so that the child does not feel the lack. So they do not experience humiliation. So they do not know frustration. So they are not "like me."

But in this effort, a distortion appears: the child is no longer seen, but compensated. They are no longer heard, but covered with things. They are no longer accompanied, but surrounded by objects.

Toys, clothes, gadgets, and vacations are bought. Everything the parent didn't have is offered, sometimes even what the child didn't ask for. Because behind every gift lies a wound. A memory. A lack.

And so, the child learns that love comes with a price—that attention must be earned, and presence is negotiated. They learn that the parent's time is scarce but can be bought: with a new tablet, a trip, a pair of expensive shoes—with anything other than authentic presence.

In the effort not to repeat the past, the parent ends up creating another type of absence: emotional absence. They are there, but not truly present. They listen, but they do not hear. They are generous, but not connected. The child receives everything—except what they truly need: a space to be seen, heard, and understood.

This motivation, though springing from love, can become a form of avoidance. The parent does not confront their pain; they cover it with gestures. They do not acknowledge their helplessness; they transform it into excess. They do not own their vulnerability; they camouflage it as generosity. But the child feels it. They feel that something is missing. They feel loved, but not understood; protected, but not known for who they truly are.

And perhaps, one day, the child will ask: "Why do you give me so much, yet I don't feel you near?" And the parent, if they have the courage to hear, will understand that love is not measured in things, but in presence. Not in gifts, but in conversations. Not in vacations, but in moments of shared silence.

Sometimes, unfulfilled dreams do not disappear. They hide in the corners of memory, in the silences between generations, in the glances that say, "I wasn't allowed." A parent who could not live out their desires—whether due to lack of resources or the absence of a safe emotional space—ends up keeping them like unsprouted seeds. And when the child arrives, those seeds are planted again, not in the parent's soul, but in the child's.

A father who, as a teenager, dreamed of playing tennis but lacked the money for equipment or the courage to tell his parents how he felt, looks at his son as a chance to rewrite the story. He buys him the best racket, enrolls him in lessons, and takes him to tournaments. At first, the child accepts. Because he loves the attention, because he feels his father's enthusiasm, because he wants to be the "good boy." But as the years pass, the sport becomes an obligation—a "mandatory elective." Practice becomes exhausting, competitions become sources of anxiety, and the joy vanishes. The child was never asked if he truly wanted this. He was never asked how he felt. What attracted him. What bored him. What hurt him.

In another family, a mother who dreamed of playing the piano but was raised in a rigid environment where art was considered useless enrolls her daughter in music lessons at age four. The girl learns quickly; she has talent, but no desire. She plays flawlessly, but without soul. She enters competitions and wins prizes, but she feels increasingly tired. She has no time to play, to explore, to breathe. And when, one day, she says she no longer wants to play the piano, the mother responds with a trembling voice: "After all the sacrifices I've made for you, you couldn't even win Competition X? You have deeply disappointed me."

This remark, spoken perhaps out of frustration or pain, becomes a wound. The child learns that love comes with conditions. That performance is the currency used to buy affection. That freedom is not a right, but a privilege that is lost if you disappoint.

And so, the child lives a life that is not their own—a life that looks beautiful on the surface but feels alien deep down. A life where they don't ask, "What do I like?" but rather, "What is expected from me?" A life in which they do not feel free, but loyal—loyal to a story that does not belong to them.

The parent, in the desire to provide what they did not receive, ends up demanding what they never asked for. And perhaps it is not their fault. Perhaps no one taught them how to heal, how to question themselves, or how to break free. But the child cannot be the space where the past is healed. They need their own path, their own questions, their own dreams.

A child also needs to see what a "budget based on saving" means. Not to be deprived of comfort, but to learn gratitude—to understand that behind every object, every fulfilled dream, every trip, or after-school activity, there is work. There are choices. There are obstacles and solutions.

When everything is handed over on a silver platter, without explanation or effort, the child learns that the world owes them—that desires are fulfilled automatically, and that "I want" is enough. But when they see a parent choosing not to buy something for themselves in order to pay for their painting class, when they take part in discussions about the family budget, or when they understand that a vacation abroad meant months of savings, they begin to see everything differently. They begin to appreciate. To respect. To contribute.

A child who learns that dreams are not fulfilled by magic, but through determination, will be less tempted to give up at the first obstacle. They will understand that the road to what they want is paved with patience, work, failures, and comebacks. They will learn that it is not shameful to say, "We cannot afford this right now"; rather, it is a lesson in planning and responsibility—an exercise in patience and resolve.

And perhaps one day, when they have their own dream—to buy a guitar, to go on an exchange program, to open a small workshop—they will know they don't have to wait for someone else to provide it. They will know they can work, save, ask for help, and build. They will know that dreams are not gifts, but projects and life goals.

A child does not need expensive clothes, shoes with shiny logos, or the latest gadgets to feel worthy. The need for brands does not come from within them; it is often projected by the parents—directly or indirectly. When a parent says, "What can I do if they see it at their classmates'?" they are actually admitting they haven't built an internal filter for discernment, but have allowed the child to be shaped by the outside world.

But a child with a solid emotional foundation, who understands who they are and what truly matters, will not feel the need to compete through appearances. They will know that their value is not measured by the label on their T-shirt, but in the way they think, feel, and act. They will learn that respect is not bought, but earned—that authenticity is rarer than any brand.

When a parent gives in to social pressure and buys expensive things "so my child doesn't feel inferior," they create a competition based on consumption, not character. The child learns they must *have*, not *be*. That they must impress, not express themselves. That they must conform, not ask themselves what truly makes them happy.

This competition is not constructive. It doesn't motivate them to grow; instead, it teaches them to compare themselves—to feel inferior for not having, to believe that love and acceptance come with a price tag. And, more seriously, it teaches them that the parent will make any sacrifice for image, rather than for substance. A child who learns to appreciate simple things (a good book, a sincere conversation, clean and comfortable clothes) will become a balanced adult. They will know how to choose what truly matters. They will know how to say, "I don't need this," without feeling like less of a person. They will know how to work for what they want, instead of waiting for it to be handed to them.

This dynamic is not necessarily conscious. The parent doesn't tell themselves, "I will live through my child." But their actions, decisions, and reactions speak for them. The choice of the child's activities reflects the parent's desires. Overreactions to the child's failure betray a personal wound. The need for control stems from the fear of reliving past pain.

It is a motivation fueled by the need for healing, yet paradoxically, it can perpetuate trauma—this time in the next generation. The child becomes an emotional trophy, a success story meant to compensate for a story of pain. But in this process, they risk losing their voice, their identity, and their freedom.

A client once told me about her childhood dream: to dance. Not just to dance, but to compete, to be acclaimed, to feel the stage beneath her feet. Years later, after becoming a mother, the dream returned to her with unexpected intensity. So, she enrolled both her children, aged 10 and 7, in ballroom dancing classes. For six months, they went to the dance center together, but every trip was a struggle. The children were hard to motivate, and enthusiasm was nowhere to be found. One day, she asked them sincerely: "Do you really want this?" The answer was clear: one wanted to paint, the other to learn karate. She realized then that the dream was hers, not theirs. And she gave up the dance classes—not with regret, but with gratitude, because she had the courage to ask, to listen, and to let go.

This choice did not mean abandoning the dream, but recognizing it as a part of her, not as a mission for someone else. My client enrolled in dance classes herself, following her dream even though she was slightly over 50.

A child is not a second chance. They are a first chance—their own. They are not a bandage for the parent's wounds, but a being with their own path, their own desires, and their own mistakes. To love them means to see them, to listen to them, and to let them be. Not to shape them after an unlived story, but to encourage them to write their own.

7.1. Implications and Consequences

When a child is entrusted with the mission of living out what the parent could not, the entire relationship is built on a fragile foundation: conditioning. Love is no longer free; it becomes an equation. The child is loved to the extent that they perform, conform to the parent's dream, and do not disappoint.

For the child, this dynamic creates a profound identity confusion. They do not know if what they do is for themselves or for someone else. They do not know if their desires belong to them or are borrowed. They do not know if failure is a personal mistake or a betrayal of a story that isn't theirs. And so, they begin to live with a silent but constant pressure: not to disappoint. Not to lose love. Not to be "less than."

This pressure manifests in subtle ways: the child accepts activities they dislike, overexerts themselves, represses authentic desires, and constantly compares themselves to others. And when they grow tired, when they want to give up, when they feel they can no longer go on, the reproaches appear: "After all the sacrifices I made for you, you couldn't even win Competition X?" This remark, spoken perhaps out of frustration or pain, becomes a wound. A wound that isn't seen, but is felt. A wound that says: "You are not enough."

For the parent, the implications are just as deep. Instead of healing, they project their pain. Instead of asking, "What did I lack and how can I come to terms with it?", they ask, "How can I make sure my child doesn't experience what I did?" But in this attempt, they lose touch with the child's reality. They no longer see them. They no longer listen. They no longer accompany them. They simply mold them according to their own will.

The parent-child relationship becomes strained, even if it appears full of affection. It is a relationship where freedom is replaced by loyalty, and authenticity by performance. The child does not feel loved for who they are, but for what they do. And the parent, though offering everything, feels they are not receiving what they expect. An invisible but deep rift is created.

At the family level, this motivation can generate imbalances: siblings are compared, resources are distributed unequally, and tensions rise. One child becomes "the project," while the other becomes "the neglected one." Resentments, silences, and distances are born.

And perhaps one day, the child will have the courage to say: "I can't do this anymore." And the parent, if they have the courage to hear, will understand that love does not mean living through someone else, but letting them live. Letting them be. Letting them make mistakes. Letting them discover themselves.

The fragile foundation of the relationship is not just about conditioning, but also about unrealistic expectations. The parent doesn't just demand performance; they project onto the child an idealized version of their own failed childhood. The child is not seen as they are, but as the parent "should have been." This projection becomes a burden.

Unrealistic expectations can take the form of impossible standards, constant comparisons with other children, or dreams that do not belong to the child. "You will be the pianist I never had the chance to be," "You will go to the university that didn't accept me," "You will have the success that I missed." Behind these statements lies unspoken pain, but also immense pressure. The child is no longer allowed to be mediocre, to make mistakes, to change their mind. They are no longer allowed to be... a child.

And thus, the relationship falters. Because it is based not on acceptance, but on projection. Not on guidance, but on redirection. Not on unconditional love, but on the hope that "this time, it will be different."

Sometimes, the parent does not impose through explicit demands, but through stories told with reproach. They remember their childhood with a heavy tone, full of pain but also of expectation. They speak of lacks, of broken dreams, of sacrifices made without recognition. "In my day, we had nothing, but I worked hard," "I had no support, but you have everything you need," "If I had your chance, I would have gone far." These words are not just memories; they are confessions delivered as reproaches. And the child listens with a lump in their throat. They feel they must compensate, repay, and not disappoint. Not out of free love, but out of guilt.

This form of transmission is perhaps the most oppressive because it leaves no room for a rebuttal. There is no clear demand, yet there is a burden. The child takes on the story as a mission. And they begin to live not just for themselves, but for the other. Not out of freedom, but out of loyalty. Not out of curiosity, but out of obligation.

But love that demands you repair someone else's past is not free love. It is love with a task. With a purpose. With a direction. And in time, the child can lose themselves in it. They may become high-achieving, admired, "successful," but hollow inside. Because they didn't live their life; they lived a story passed down with pain and pressure.

Sometimes, the parent-child relationship is not marked by open conflict, but by coldness, distance, and heavy silences. It is a relationship where the child feels they must be careful with every word, every gesture, as if they are walking on eggshells. There is no open, free communication, only functional interaction devoid of warmth. The parent may be physically present, but emotionally they are far away—preoccupied, fearful, critical, or simply unavailable.

In this climate, the child does not feel safe being vulnerable. They do not dare to ask, to make mistakes, or to express themselves. And so, they begin to hide. They withdraw their thoughts, repress their emotions, and build an inner world where they can breathe. And when the need for exploration becomes too strong, they do it on their own—without guidance, without support, without landmarks.

In the absence of a supportive relationship, the child will seek acceptance outside the family. And sometimes, they will find it in the wrong circles, where they are not judged, where they can be "themselves," even if that "self" is confused, wounded, or adrift. Because the need for belonging is stronger than fear. And if there is no room for authenticity at home, the child will seek it anywhere else.

This dynamic is not always visible. From the outside, the family may seem "normal." But on the inside, the child lives with constant tension, a lack of validation, and a mute pain. And in time, this pain can turn into rebellion, isolation, or even self-destruction.

7.2. Alternatives and Reflections

Projecting a parent's unfulfilled dreams onto a child can seem, in moments of vulnerability, like a form of hope—a continuation, a repair. But this choice, if not accompanied by a deep awareness, risks transforming the child into a vehicle for the past, rather than a free being. Consequently, the relationship becomes a pre-written script instead of a living space for connection.

There are alternatives that do not deny these desires but place them in context—alternatives that do not demand renunciation, but maturity; that do not impose but release:

· Processing unfulfilled dreams within a therapeutic framework. Before asking a child to follow a certain path, a parent needs to understand why that path matters to them. What part of their self is hoping to be validated? What wound is crying out for recognition? Unfulfilled dreams do not have to disappear, but neither should they become transmitted burdens. Understanding them is the first step toward liberation.

- Separating the parent's identity from that of the child. The child is not an extension. They are not a second chance at a "rematch" with life. They are a being with their own rhythms, choices, and limits. Seeing them for who they are, rather than who we hope they will become, is an act of mature love. It means accompanying them, not leading them.
- Building a relationship based on curiosity, not projection. Asking "What are you passionate about?" instead of "Do you want to do what I did?" Listening without correcting. Observing without comparing. Being there without conditioning. The relationship is built in the present, not in the echo of the past.
- Discussing dreams with one's partner. Sometimes, projections come from both directions. It is essential for parents to honestly express their desires, fears, and ideals. They should ask each other: "What part of us are we hoping to live out through our child?" The child is not a joint project, but a being who deserves space, not a forced direction.
- Exploring personal dreams outside the role of a parent. Unfulfilled dreams can be resumed, rewritten, or reimagined through personal projects, passions, or community. Being a parent does not mean giving up on oneself, but learning to express oneself without conditioning someone else. The child should not be the sole source of meaning.
- Building a solid relationship based on trust and authenticity. A solid relationship is not built on performance, but on presence—on the ability to be there, day by day, with patience,

listening, and availability. A child needs to feel they are loved for who they are, not for who they might become; that they can fail without losing affection and say “no” without being rejected. A solid relationship is one where the child feels seen, not evaluated—where they can explore without being pushed and be themselves without being compared.

- Returning to the past as a form of connection, not pressure. Stories about the parent’s childhood can become a meeting ground rather than a point of comparison. Told in a gentle tone of acceptance and vulnerability, they can spark the child’s curiosity instead of a fear of disappointing. “In my day...” should not be a judgment, but a window into another world—a story that does not demand replication, but offers understanding. When a parent shares their history as a part of themselves rather than a mandatory model, the child learns that the past can be honored without being repeated.
- Creating family meetings dedicated to authentic listening. In a hurried world where screens separate us more than they bring us together, a family needs sacred moments of reconnection—meetings where phones are turned off and attention is turned on. In these moments, every member is invited to speak openly about dreams, fears, successes, shames, and needs. Without judgment. Without interruptions. Without pressure. Only presence. These conversations do not have to be perfect, but real. They can become a ritual of collective healing, where the child learns that their voice matters, and the parent discovers that vulnerability does not weaken the relationship, but strengthens it. To truly connect

means being willing to listen not only to what is said, but also to what remains unspoken.

Reflection Questions

- What were my own unfulfilled dreams from childhood?
- Which unfulfilled dream do I hope will live on through my child?
- Do I see them for who they are, or for who I hope they will become?
- What part of me is seeking validation through their success?
- How can I show that my child's path can be different from my own?
- How can I express my own desires without projecting them onto my child?
- What space am I offering my child to discover themselves on their own?
- What can I do today to live my own meaning, without imposing it on someone else?
- What part of my past can be shared as a lesson, rather than a direction?
- When was the last time I truly listened—without correcting, without rushing, and without judging?

Chapter 8

Unhealthy Motivation 6: The Child who Saves the Relationship

„A child is not a project. He represents a relationship".

Jesper Juul

There are moments in a couple's life when silence becomes heavier than any argument. When eyes avoid each other, when words are spoken only out of obligation, and when touch turns into routine. When there is a minimal conversation just for the sake of it. When the silence hurts and you feel you have exhausted every topic. Something has broken, but it remains unsaid. Something hurts, but it is not acknowledged. And in this space of silence and fear, an idea emerges that seems like a lifesaver: "Maybe a child will bring us closer." It is a hope born out of the need for reconnection, out of the desire to save what seems lost. But it is also a form of avoidance—avoiding confrontation, honesty, and uncomfortable questions. The child becomes, without knowing it, the solution. The glue. The common mission meant to repair what is no longer spoken.

This motivation is not always conscious. Sometimes it comes as a "natural" desire to start a family. Other times it appears as a rushed decision after an argument, a temporary breakup, or an emotional crisis. But deep down, the child is entrusted with an impossible task: to heal a relationship that can no longer sustain itself. They are not wanted for who they will be, but for what they might do. They are seen as a joint project, a unifying responsibility, a pretext for staying together. Like a lifebuoy thrown into a sea that no longer has a shore.

But the child feels it. They feel the tension, the silence, the sense that something is wrong. They hear the arguments and reproaches in the background; they hear the parents' sighs. And, without understanding why, they begin to believe they are either the cause or the solution. That they must be "good," "perfect," "unproblematic," so as not to aggravate the rift. They live with a silent pressure: not to disappoint, not to make things worse, not to lose love. They become attentive to every nuance, every exchange of glances between the parents, every silence that stretches too long. And when the silence settles in, they try to create conversation, to fill the empty space. They learn to read others' emotions before understanding their own. They learn to adapt, to hide, to avoid being a bother—to survive.

And perhaps the parents, instead of coming closer, drift even further apart. Because they avoided the truth instead of confronting it. Because they built over the cracks instead of repairing them. Because they put a child between them, not beside them. And the child grows up with a profound confusion: "If I hadn't been here, would it have been better? Or worse?" They wonder if the love between their parents is real or just a convention. They wonder if they are the reason why they stayed, or the reason why they didn't leave. It is cruel and painful to live with such turmoil, with constant uncertainty.

She and he. Two people who once loved each other passionately. Now, they look at each other like strangers. In the kitchen, the silence is heavier than any argument. In the bedroom, the distance is colder than any breakup. And yet, one evening, after a tear-filled discussion, she says: "Maybe if we had a child, things would change." He doesn't answer immediately. But in his eyes, one can read hope. Or fear. Or both.

The child arrives. With their smile, their needs, their light. But the relationship does not heal. It transforms into a logistical partnership. Into an exchange of responsibilities. Into a "you take the kid to daycare, I'll do the groceries." Love does not reignite. It just hides better. The child grows. And they feel it. They feel that their parents no longer love each other. They feel they are between them, not with them. They feel they must be "good" so as not to lose them.

This unhealthy motivation—having a child to save a relationship—creates a fragile dynamic where love becomes conditional and the child's identity is built upon a mission that is not theirs. They do not feel loved for who they are, but for what they provide. They do not feel free to make mistakes, to express themselves, or to be authentic. Because they feel the family's balance depends on them. And in future relationships, they will seek love with that same pressure: to be "enough," to be a "savior," to be "the reason why someone stays."

A child should not be the glue of a relationship. They should not be the reason two people stay together. They should not be the solution to a rift. They deserve to be wanted for who they are, not for what they can fix. They deserve to be loved unconditionally, not entrusted with a silent mission. They deserve to be free, not responsible for the happiness of others.

And perhaps true salvation does not come from a new start, but from the courage to look at what has been lost. From the sincerity of admitting that love is no longer felt. From the maturity of understanding that a child is not a solution, but a being who deserves to be welcomed with a whole heart, not with the hope that they will fill the voids left by others.

Sometimes, a child is not just a hope for the present, but also an attempt to heal the past. One parent (or both) carries old wounds—misunderstandings with their own parents, unfulfilled loves, silent abandonments. And then, the child becomes more than a new life: they become a chance to do things "the right way." To fix what was left unsaid or undone. To live, through them, an ideal version of one's own childhood. But this projection, however well-intentioned, turns the child into an instrument of personal healing. They are not given the freedom to be who they are; instead, a path is laid out for them: to be happier, more balanced, more "correct" than their parents were. To not repeat their mistakes. To be the proof that the parents have learned, grown, and become "better."

In such relationships, the child is not only the glue between parents but also the bridge between generations. They become a transgenerational repair project. The pressure comes not only from the present but from the unspoken past. The child feels they must be the "result" of a lesson, not a free being—that they must confirm the parents made the right choices, that they weren't wrong to stay together, or to bring them into the world.

Later, as an adult, this child may become someone who doesn't know who they are without others. Someone who feels they must be "useful" in every relationship. They define themselves through roles—son, partner, friend, support—but not through essence. Not through freedom. They may become an adult who cannot afford to be vulnerable, to withdraw, or to say "no." Because they learned early on that their existence must be justified. That love is earned. That presence is negotiated.

And perhaps, one day, they will feel a void they cannot explain. An exhaustion that doesn't come from work, but from the constant effort of being "enough." A sadness that has no cause, only roots. And they will begin to search. To wonder. To go back in time. To understand that they were loved, but not free. That they were wanted, but not for who they were. That they were chosen, but not seen.

The child who comes to save a relationship is not just a child. They are a story where desires, fears, needs, and pasts intermingle. They are a mirror in which parents project what they haven't lived, said, or healed. But they deserve more than to be a bridge. They deserve to be their own path. They deserve to be the beginning of a story, not the continuation of a wandering.

In moments of crisis, when the relationship falters and the soul is weary of arguments and silences, the need for support arises. The couple looks for answers outside themselves: from parents, friends, or close ones who seem to know better. But every piece of advice comes through the filter of a life lived differently, through personal experience and a past that does not resemble yours—not through an objective viewpoint. When you are vulnerable, disoriented, and saturated with conflict, you no longer have the strength to filter. You receive those words as revelations, turn them into solutions, and follow them without asking what you truly want or what suits you. Some mothers advise their daughters: "Maybe it's time to have a child. That way you give your husband some responsibility, and you'll see he'll come around." But that advice isn't about your relationship; it's about her fears and hopes. It's not about what you feel, but about what she lived. And thus, the child becomes not a choice, but a strategy. An attempt to fix something that wasn't understood. A decision made not out of love, but out of exhaustion. The result is not closeness, but a new form of distance—one that bears the face of a child who never asked to be the bridge between two lost souls.

When a relationship goes well, it's because both contributed. When it goes poorly, it's also because both contributed. The truth is simple, yet hard to face. And that is precisely why the idea that a child could bring the relationship closer—that they could solve problems they didn't create—becomes a subtle form of avoidance. It is a displacement of responsibility onto a being who has neither the power, the context, nor the choice. Instead of asking, "What did I do to get us here?", we ask, "What could someone else do to get us out of here?" It is a lack of accountability masked as hope. A flight from responsibility packaged as a desire for reconstruction. But children do not learn from what we tell them; they learn from what we do. The power of example is magical and dangerous (especially when you lack the strength to see that this is what you have sown). If a parent does not take ownership of their contribution to a problematic context, the child will learn that avoidance is normal. That guilt can be shifted. That solutions come from the outside, not from within. And they will replicate the model.

They will become the adult who doesn't ask, "What did I do?", but "Who can fix what I broke?" The lesson passed down is not about love, but about delegation. Not about maturity, but about illusion. Thus, the child doesn't save the relationship; they learn to live in relationships that aren't saved, but avoided.

How can someone else find solutions to problems you created? This is a question that should lie at the heart of any mature decision. Because every choice, every reaction, every silence or word spoken in a relationship has a consequence. And those consequences do not disappear if we ignore them; they do not dissolve if we delegate them. Placing them on someone else's shoulders—whether a child, a partner, or an external "solution"—means refusing to look in the mirror. This should not be confused with the idea of asking for help. Asking for help is an act of courage, of ownership, of openness. But expecting someone else to fix what you broke, without understanding your own role, is a subtle form of avoidance. It is like letting someone else pay the bill for a dinner where you chose the menu.

The child, in this context, is not the help requested, but the responsibility projected. They are not the conscious support, but the imagined magical solution. And so, instead of learning about accountability, cause and effect, and maturity, the child learns that problems can be passed on, that guilt can be displaced, and that presence can substitute for responsibility. The lesson transmitted is not about love, but about avoidance. Not about healing, but about delegation. And they will carry this model forward, never knowing it was never truly theirs.

How can you believe a child will grow in a healthy, harmonious environment conducive to development when the very foundation of that environment is unstable, cracked, and lacking emotional coherence? It is like planting a flower in sandy soil—without nutrients, water, or light—and expecting it to bloom continuously, regardless of the season. A child is not a magical entity that transcends the context into which they are born. They absorb everything: the unspoken tensions, the untreated fears, the lack of meaning, direction, and authentic love. Growth does not happen in a vacuum. It requires roots, stability, and constant care. If the environment they enter is toxic, chaotic, or built on a lack of accountability, the child will not learn to bloom, but to survive. They will learn to adapt, to shrink, to protect themselves. And that is not development; it is defense. Not harmony, but compromise. Not love, but confusion. Hoping a child will become whole in a fragmented context is a dangerous illusion. Because not only the child suffers, but also the generations to come, silently carrying wounds that do not belong to them.

8.1. Implications and Consequences

The decision to bring a child into the world for the purpose of saving a relationship is, in essence, a way of avoiding the truth. Instead of confronting the real difficulties of the relationship (lack of communication, unfulfilled needs, emotional distancing), parents choose to project their hope onto a future that does not belong entirely to them: the child. This choice, though it may seem full of good intentions, generates profound and often painful consequences.

The child, born into a tense context, involuntarily becomes a symbol of reconciliation. They are not viewed simply as an autonomous being, but as a bond, a solution, a justification. In a family environment saturated with arguments, reproaches, and heavy silences, the child learns early on that love is conditional. They feel they must be "good," "well-behaved," "unproblematic," so as not to aggravate the rift between their parents. Every argument makes them wonder if they are the cause—if their presence is the reason why their parents are suffering. No one tells them this directly, but they feel it. And they begin to adapt. They shrink emotionally; they avoid asking, crying, or making mistakes. They live with a silent pressure: not to disappoint, not to be a cause of conflict, not to lose love.

Over time, this pressure transforms into anxiety, low self-esteem, and relationship difficulties. The child doesn't understand why love feels unstable, but they feel it nonetheless. And they will replicate it. As an adult, they may become someone who doesn't know who they are without others, someone who feels they must be "useful" in every relationship, defining themselves through roles rather than essence. They may become an adult who cannot afford to be vulnerable, to withdraw, or to say "no," because they learned early on that their very existence must be justified.

For the parents, the implications are just as profound. Instead of drawing closer, they may drift even further apart. The child, instead of being a free being, becomes a joint project, a mission, a hope. The relationship does not heal; it becomes more complicated. It transforms into a logistical partnership, an exchange of responsibilities, a routine that masks the lack of connection. Love does not reignite; it only hides better. Arguments become more frequent, more intense, and more laden with frustration. Each parent projects their unfulfillment onto the other, and the child becomes the silent witness to a relationship unraveling before their eyes.

The mother may feel she has been emotionally abandoned, left to carry the weight of a decision that brought no healing. The father may feel pushed into a role that doesn't fit him, having lost the freedom to choose. Both parents may sense the failure, yet they rarely verbalize it. Instead, tension accumulates, and the child absorbs it like toxic air.

In such an environment, the child does not learn what a healthy relationship looks like—one based on respect, communication, and accountability. They learn that love is earned, presence is negotiated, and peace is a temporary privilege. They do not feel free to explore, to make mistakes, or to be authentic. They hide, protect themselves, and adapt. Inside them, a latent guilt is born, along with an acute need for validation and an identity built on performance rather than freedom.

In some cases, after a long period of tension and misunderstanding, the parents end up divorcing. This rupture, while potentially a liberation, comes with a major emotional cost. For the parents, divorce does not automatically mean healing. The unhealed wound retreats, hiding beneath the appearance of a new start. Without real introspection, they may unconsciously choose relationships similar to those in the past—relationships that repeat the same patterns of avoidance, lack of accountability, and conflict. When difficulties arise, they prefer to end the relationship rather than repair it, because they never learned how to confront, how to build, or how to stay.

For the child, the parents' divorce is often felt as a personal failure. If they were entrusted with the role of "glue," "solution," or "mission," then the parents' separation becomes proof that they failed. Not only is the family falling apart, but the very meaning of their existence seems to collapse. They may feel useless, guilty, and abandoned. They carry the idea that they weren't good enough, that they couldn't keep them together, that their love wasn't sufficient. This unspoken but profound experience can mark their entire emotional and relational development.

In this context, the child not only suffers from the separation but also internalizes a dysfunctional model of relating. They learn that relationships are unstable, love is lost, and people leave. As an adult, they may become either excessively attached, fearing abandonment, or distant, unable to engage emotionally. They may avoid conflict at all costs or, conversely, unconsciously provoke it, because that is the only dynamic they know. It becomes a kind of test to see who will stay by their side.

Once they reach adulthood, this child will unconsciously seek to repair what they failed to save in their own family. They will engage in "reparative relationships," taking on the role of savior, supporter, or healer. They will attract fragile, unstable partners in crisis, because in that dynamic, they feel competent, necessary, and valuable. They will not understand what it means to live for themselves, to choose themselves, or to build a life that is not based on saving others. They will confuse love with sacrifice, presence with duty, and commitment with self-abandonment.

This tendency can also be reflected in professional choices. It is highly likely that an adult formed in this context will lean toward fields involving the saving of others (psychology, medicine, social work, education, volunteering)—not just out of vocation, but out of a deep need to fix what they could not fix in their own childhood. Choosing these professions can be noble, but if not accompanied by awareness and healing, it risks perpetuating an identity built on pain rather than freedom.

The choice to bring a child into the world to save a relationship is not just a personal decision; it is one with major ethical and psychological implications. It affects the child's emotional development, the quality of the couple's relationship, and long-term family health. A child deserves to be wanted for who they are, not for what they can fix. They deserve to be loved unconditionally, not entrusted with a silent mission. They deserve to be free, not responsible for the emotional balance of those who brought them into the world.

8.2. Alternatives and Reflections

Bringing a child into the world with the hope that they will save a relationship may seem, in moments of despair, like a gesture of love. An attempt. A bridge. But this choice, if not accompanied by a profound sense of accountability, risks transforming the child into a silent mediator, a forced bond, and a witness to a relationship that cannot heal itself. Consequently, the family becomes a space of tension rather than growth.

There are alternatives that do not deny the desire to stay together but instead ground it in truth—alternatives that do not flee from the rift but confront it with maturity; that do not demand silent sacrifices, but rather openness and responsibility:

- Honestly confronting the reality of the relationship. Before bringing a child into the relationship, partners need to ask themselves: "Are we here out of love or out of fear?", "What keeps us together?", "What are we missing?". Acknowledging the cracks doesn't mean destroying the bond, but clarifying it. Relationships are not repaired through avoidance, but through spoken truths.

- Seeking therapeutic support. Couple's therapy provides a safe space where partners can learn to communicate, listen, and understand each other beyond their immediate reactions. It is an act of responsibility, not just toward the relationship, but toward the child who might be brought into the world. Asking for help doesn't mean the relationship is doomed; it means it deserves a real chance.
- Conscious separation, when reconstruction is not possible. Sometimes, parting ways is the most mature form of love. Staying together out of fear or guilt does not protect the child; it burdens them. Conscious separation involves respect, clarity, and care for oneself and the other. It is a choice that can prevent the perpetuation of suffering.
- Individual reconstruction for the parents. After a breakup, parents need time and space to understand which patterns they repeated, which wounds they avoided, and why they chose certain relationships. Without this introspection, they risk attracting unsuitable partners again, fleeing from difficulties, or ending things before truly trying. Healing does not come from forgetting, but from understanding.
- Redefining one's personal role in relationships. The child-turned-adult, who grew up with the mission to "save" the family, needs to learn they do not have to fix anyone to be loved—that they can live for themselves, not through others. Love is not a mission; it is a free choice. Letting go of the "savior" role is an act of profound liberation.

- Becoming aware of professional choices as a reflection of the past. Many adults raised as mediators choose "saving" professions (psychology, medicine, education, social work, etc.). These choices can be noble, but it is essential they aren't the sole source of validation. Saving should not be an identity, but a free vocation born out of balance, not pain.
- Limiting the influence of subjective external advice. In moments of crisis, parents may be tempted to seek answers from those around them—friends, family, or acquaintances. But the advice received, however well-intentioned, is filtered through personal experiences, unresolved emotions, and private beliefs. What worked for someone else is no guarantee it will work for everyone. Furthermore, some advice can inflame the situation, amplify guilt, or encourage rushed decisions. It is recommended that parents turn to objective sources, professional counseling, personal reflection, and authentic dialogue, avoiding as much as possible the pressure of advice that ignores the uniqueness of their own relationship.
- Building an authentic relationship with the child based on freedom and presence. If the child is already present, parents can choose to release them from the role of the "glue." To see them for who they are, not for what they hope to fix. To offer them space, not pressure. To allow them to make mistakes, to explore, and to be themselves. The relationship can heal through authenticity, not control.
- Creating a family space for listening and vulnerability. Instead of tension, the family can become a place of true connection—meetings where every member is invited to speak about what they feel, what hurts, and what scares them.

Without judgment. Without interruption. Without conditions. These moments can become rituals of reconnection, where the child learns that their voice matters, and the parent discovers that vulnerability does not weaken the relationship but strengthens it. Moreover, the parent can see, in real-time, how their child perceives their love and involvement.

Reflection Questions

- What part of my relationship do I hope will be saved through the child?
- What are the difficulties I am currently facing in my couple?
- What solutions can my partner and I identify together for our difficulties?
- What am I avoiding confronting in my relationship and instead projecting onto the family's future?
- Am I willing to look honestly at what isn't working?
- What does a mature, accountable relationship mean to me?
- How can I build a relationship where the child is not a mediator, but a free being?
- What patterns do I repeat in relationships, and how can I understand them?
- What does it mean for me to live for myself, rather than through others?
- How did I choose my profession: out of vocation or out of a need to repair the past?
- How can I release my child from the role of a savior?

- What external advice has influenced me, and how can I filter it with discernment?
- When was the last time I truly listened—without correcting, without rushing, and without judging?

Chapter 9

Unhealthy Motivation 7: The Child for Social Benefits

"Children are not the property of their parents. They do not exist to satisfy their parents' needs."

Alice Miller

There are moments when the decision to bring a child into the world is not born out of an impulse of love, but out of a need for survival. In a world where social systems offer support to those who become parents—where child allowances, social housing, and priority access to services become bargaining chips—the child risks being transformed into a means, not an end. They are not wanted for who they are, but for the benefits they can bring.

This motivation is not always malicious or cynical. Sometimes, it is desperate. Other times, it is learned. In vulnerable communities, in environments where deprivation is chronic, motherhood becomes a strategy. It is not a conscious choice, but a way to obtain a minimum level of stability. Young women, sometimes teenagers, are encouraged to become mothers not because they are ready, but because "that's how it's done," because "otherwise you have nowhere to stay," because "with a child, the state helps you."

But the child is not blind to the motivation that brought them into the world. Even if they cannot articulate it, they feel it. They feel they are not looked upon with admiration, but with expectation. That they are not listened to, but accounted for. That they are not accompanied, but used. And this feeling becomes a silent wound that deepens over time, transforming into the conviction that their value is conditional.

A child raised for social benefits learns early on that their existence is tied to paperwork. To allowances. To visits to various institutions. To justifications. To deadlines. To applications. They are not told about dreams, but about forms. They are not asked what they feel, but what they must do. This is a child who becomes an adult before their time—not because they are mature, but because they are artificially burdened with responsibility. They must be "good," "so they don't cut our aid," "so they don't get in our way."

This dynamic creates a parental relationship where love is replaced by functionality. The parent does not ask, "What does my child need?" but "What must I do so I don't lose the support?" The child becomes an administrative project, not a being in the making. And in this relationship, affection is rarely unconditional.

As the child grows, the idea that they must be grateful is instilled in them. Not for love, but for their very existence. "If it weren't for you, we would have nothing," "I did everything for you," "You are the reason we received help." These statements, though seemingly positive, are laden with pressure. The child does not feel free to make mistakes, to explore, or to rebel. They feel they must compensate. To be “good.” To not disappoint. To not lose what was obtained through them.

This burden of gratitude becomes a subtle form of control. The child is not loved for who they are, but for what they provide. And when they no longer provide—when they grow up, become autonomous, and no longer bring in benefits—the relationship cools. It transforms. It becomes conditional. And the child is left with the question: “If I am no longer useful, am I still loved?”

It is vital to also look at the system that makes this motivation possible. Social benefits are essential, but when they become the sole reason for bringing a child into the world, it means something is missing. Education. Emotional support. Counseling. Healthy role models. Accountability. A society that offers aid but fails to provide guidance risks creating generations of children raised in the absence of authentic intention.

A child is not a solution to a lack of resources. They are not an access route. They are not a justification. They are a being who deserves to be wanted, not used. They deserve to be accompanied, not conditioned. They deserve to be loved, not accounted for.

In Romania, state child allowances remain among the lowest in the European Union. At approximately 290 lei per month (around 58–60 euros) for children between 2 and 18, the support provided by the state is often insufficient to cover a child’s real needs. In contrast, countries like Germany offer up to 250–297 euros per month per child, while France, Italy, or Austria have progressive systems that increase the allowance based on the number of children or family income. This financial discrepancy has led to an increasingly visible phenomenon: Romanian parents choosing to temporarily relocate to other European states, especially where legislation allows access to child benefits even for temporary residents. Thus, the child becomes not just a source of internal support, but a "social passport" for external benefits. It is a choice that, while it may seem pragmatic, raises profound questions about parental intention, affective migration, and the way social systems shape the intimate decisions of the family.

It is deeply unsettling and disheartening to observe how, in some cases, the decision to have a child is not linked to love, maturity, or the desire to accompany a developing being, but to a cold, unaccountable calculation: obtaining social benefits. It is a choice that betrays not only the child but the very essence of adult responsibility. Instead of taking ownership of their lives, seeking their place in the world, identifying a job, becoming employed, and actively contributing to their own existence, some parents choose to live on social welfare, transforming the child into a source of income rather than a being to be loved. It is a form of moral abandonment, a flight from maturity, an avoidance of effort and personal growth. In this equation, the child becomes a bargaining chip, a pretext, a justification for stagnation. This choice not only deprives the child of authentic affection but also burdens them with an unfair load: that of involuntarily supporting a family that has not taken ownership of its life, but merely its existence.

In recent years, an increasingly visible phenomenon has emerged among young people: the rush to marry and have a child, not out of an authentic desire to start a family or out of love, but out of a pragmatic calculation linked to social benefits. Government programs offer state-guaranteed loans for young newlyweds, with subsidized interest rates and advantageous conditions for purchasing a home, organizing a wedding, or continuing studies. In this context, the child unfortunately becomes an "eligibility criterion" for obtaining material advantages: a discounted house, priority for a job, a chance at professional stability. It is a reality that, although supported by positive government intentions, can be derailed by a lack of personal accountability.

When a child is brought into the world as a key to social doors, rather than a being to be accompanied, the profound meaning of motherhood and fatherhood is lost. Responsibility is lost. Unconditional love is lost. And the child, raised in a framework where their existence is justified by advantages rather than affection, will carry a painful question in their soul: "Was I wanted, or was I just necessary?"

9.1. Implications and Consequences

When a child is brought into the world as a means of obtaining social benefits, the entire family structure is built upon a fragile motivation, devoid of emotional depth. There is no authentic intention to accompany a new life, only a need for financial support, access to housing, or administrative validation. This choice, though it may appear pragmatic, generates profound, painful, and often irreversible consequences.

For parents, the implications are manifold. First and foremost, a form of avoidance regarding adult responsibility sets in. Instead of taking ownership of their lives—seeking employment or pursuing personal and professional development—the parent takes refuge in the status of a "beneficiary." The child becomes the justification for stagnation, for the lack of evolution, and the absence of accountability. Over time, this dynamic generates frustration and resentment, not because the social support is insufficient, but because a life lived through someone else cannot bring fulfillment. The parent feels trapped in a role they did not fully understand but chose out of a need for survival. When the child does not "deliver"—does not behave exemplarily, bring peace, or justify the benefits—tensions, reproaches, and emotional distancing arise.

For the child, the implications are even more profound. From their earliest years, they feel that their presence is tied to a function, not to love. They are not asked how they feel, but what they must do. They are not accompanied; they are conditioned. They live in an environment where affection is replaced by utility, and the freedom to explore is replaced by the pressure not to "ruin" the family's fragile balance. The child learns that their value is tied to what they provide, not who they are. This learning becomes the foundation of an identity built on performance, conformity, and the fear of disappointment.

As an adult, this child carries a silent wound: the conviction that they must be useful to be loved. they engage in relationships where they take on the role of savior, supporter, or pillar. They choose professions involving helping others—not just out of vocation, but out of a deep need to repair what they could not fix in their own childhood. They do not know what it means to live for themselves, to choose themselves, or to build a life that is not based on saving others. They confuse love with sacrifice, presence with duty, and commitment with self-abandonment.

In this context, the parent-child relationship is marked by imbalance. It is built on dependency, not trust; on functionality, not authenticity. The parent does not see the child as a developing being, but as a source of income. And the child does not feel free to be themselves, but responsible for the family's stability. This relationship allows no room for vulnerability, does not encourage exploration, and does not support individuality. It is a relationship where love is conditional and freedom is negotiated.

At a social level, this dynamic creates a rift between the system's intent and lived reality. Social benefits are designed as forms of support, not as motivations for procreation. But when they become an end in themselves, the profound meaning of social policy is lost. Families are created where the child is an eligibility criterion, not an affective choice. Dependency is perpetuated instead of autonomy. Stagnation is encouraged instead of development. Society, instead of supporting evolution, ends up sustaining a form of survival that brings neither dignity nor fulfillment.

The implications are therefore systemic. They affect the individual, the family, and the community. Most gravely, they affect the child—the one who did not choose to be there, but who will carry the entire weight of a decision made out of lack, not love.

In some cases, as the first children grow and pass the eligible age for certain social benefits, parents face a reality they have not prepared for: the loss of financial support. Lacking a job, a qualification, or a strategy for autonomy, they remain in a state of dependency—a profound reversal of natural roles. The child, who should have been supported by the parents, ends up supporting them. And the parent, instead of rising, chooses to restart the cycle: they have another child, not out of a desire to love, but out of a need to survive.

This choice is not merely individual; it is systemic. It reflects a lack of parental education, an absence of real support for professional reintegration, and a social policy that, while well-intentioned, can be exploited. The child becomes, once again, an instrument, not a being. And the family transforms into a mechanism for obtaining resources, not a space for growth and flourishing.

The consequences are severe:

- For parents, dependency deepens, and any motivation for growth is lost. They no longer see work as a source of dignity, but see the child as a source of income.
- For older children, a form of alienation emerges: they understand they were "useful" up to a certain point, and now they are being replaced. They feel abandoned, unimportant, and pushed out of the center of attention.
- For the new child, the same scenario repeats: they are brought into the world with a function, not a meaning. They will experience the same pressure, the same conditioning, and the same lack of freedom.
- For the parent-child relationship, a rift sets in: love becomes transactional, and trust disappears. Children begin to see their parents not as role models, but as beneficiaries of their own existence.
- For society, a form of stagnation is perpetuated: instead of supporting development, the system ends up sustaining a dependency that has no resolution.

This dynamic is, in essence, a form of survival that feeds off someone else's future. And perhaps the most tragic part is that this "someone else" is a child: a being who did not choose to be there, but who will carry the entire weight of a decision made out of lack, not out of love.

9.2. Alternatives and Reflections

Bringing a child into the world to obtain social benefits may seem, in moments of vulnerability, like a pragmatic solution. A strategy. A form of survival. But this choice, if not accompanied by a profound sense of accountability, risks transforming the child into a means, rather than an end. An instrument of validation, rather than a free being. Consequently, the family becomes a space of transaction rather than growth. The child is not seen for who they are, but for what they can provide. And the parent, instead of rising, leans upon a being who did not choose to carry this burden.

There are alternatives that do not deny the difficulty but instead confront it with maturity—alternatives that do not flee from deprivation but transform it into motivation; that do not demand silent sacrifices, but rather openness, responsibility, and courage:

- Honestly confronting one's own reality. Before bringing a child into the world, it is essential for the adult to ask: "What am I truly missing?", "What do I hope to solve through this child?", "What can I not sustain on my own?". Acknowledging need is not a sign of weakness, but the beginning of maturity. A child cannot fill voids that the parent has not first understood.
- Accessing professional support. There are training programs, psychological counseling, and community initiatives that can support an adult in the process of reconstruction. Asking for help is not an act of dependency, but of responsibility. It is a way of saying: "I want to be prepared to give, not just to ask."
- Breaking the repetitive cycle of dependency. If the first children were brought into the world to obtain financial support, and this support disappears as they grow, the solution

is not the birth of another child. This is the moment when the parent can choose to rise, to learn, to work, and to reconnect with their own dignity. Having a child to maintain an income is a form of avoidance, not accountability.

- Limiting the influence of subjective external advice. In moments of crisis, parents may be tempted to follow advice that seems like a lifesaver but ignores the uniqueness of their own life. It is essential that decisions are made through reflection, not pressure—out of discernment, not imitation.
- Building an authentic relationship with the child based on freedom and presence. If the child is already present, the parent can choose to release them from the role of a supporter. To see them for who they are, not for what they bring. To offer them space, not conditioning. To allow them to make mistakes, to explore, and to be themselves. The relationship can heal through authenticity, not control.
- Creating a family space for listening and vulnerability. Instead of tension, the family can become a place of true connection—meetings where every member is invited to speak about what they feel, what hurts, and what scares them. Without judgment. Without interruption. Without conditions. These moments can become rituals of reconnection, where the child learns that their voice matters, and the parent discovers that vulnerability does not weaken the relationship but strengthens it.
- Reconstructing personal identity. The parent needs to see themselves beyond the role of a "beneficiary." To remember who they are, what they are capable of, and what they dream of. The child needs to see themselves beyond the role of a

"supporter"—to understand they do not have to be useful to be loved. Society, in turn, needs to support this reconstruction not through conditions, but through encouragement.

- Mentorship and personal development programs. Initiatives dedicated to children from vulnerable backgrounds can become spaces of profound transformation. They do not just offer educational activities; they create contexts where the child is seen, heard, and validated. Through mentorship, the child has the chance to interact with an adult who does not judge or condition them, but accompanies them. A mentor can become the first figure to ask: "What do you like?", "What do you dream of?", "What do you need to grow?"—questions often missing from a family environment marked by survival.
- Psychological counseling and emotional support. Healing personal trauma is not a luxury, but a necessity, especially when a child's life is at stake. Many parents who choose to have a child out of financial need carry old wounds: abandonment, lack of affection, dysfunctional parental models, shame, and mistrust. Without awareness, these traumas are passed down—subtly, but constantly. The child becomes the recipient of a pain that does not belong to them. Counseling offers a safe space where the adult can learn to recognize their emotions, understand their reactions, and reframe their beliefs about themselves and the world. It is the place where the parent can speak, cry, and learn to forgive themselves. This healing not only liberates the parent but creates an environment where the child can grow without being an extension of the parent's pain.

- Building a support network. In moments of vulnerability, isolation is the most dangerous ally. Many parents close themselves off in shame, in silence, and in the conviction that they must manage alone. But no one grows in the absence of relationships. Communities, relatives, and friends can become sources of real support—not just financial, but emotional, informational, and directional. Sometimes, a sincere conversation with a trusted person can open unexpected paths. Other times, a recommendation, an encouragement, or a simple question ("How can I help you?") can change the perspective of a parent in a impasse.

Reflection Questions

- What do I hope to gain through this child, and what am I avoiding confronting within myself?
- What part of my life have I put on hold, hoping that a child would resolve it?
- What does being a parent mean to me: being a supporter or being a beneficiary?
- What patterns am I repeating, and how can I understand them before passing them on?
- What alternatives do I have to being dependent on social support?
- What resources exist around me that I haven't explored yet?
- What does an authentic relationship with my child mean to me?
- How can I release my child from the role of a supporter?

- What external advice has influenced me, and how can I filter it with discernment?
- When was the last time I truly listened—without correcting, without rushing, and without judging?
- What does it mean for me to live for myself, rather than through others?
- What prevents me from believing that I can build an independent life for my child?

Chapter 10

Unhealthy Motivation 8: The Child who Gives Life a Meaning

"Nothing has a stronger psychological influence on the child than the unlived life of the parent."
Carl Jung

There is a form of love that seems sacred, but which, when viewed through a therapeutic lens, hides a profound wound: the love that transforms the child into the very meaning of life.

Here is a phrase I often hear in my practice: "If it weren't for my child, I don't know what would have become of me." It is a declaration that seems full of love, but upon closer inspection, it hides a massive burden. Because when a child becomes an adult's reason for living, they are no longer just a child. They become a lighthouse, a mission, a salvation, a justification. And that, as poetic as it may sound, is not love—it is projection.

The need for meaning is one of the deepest human needs. When life wounds us, when relationships crumble, when dreams collapse, we instinctively look for a foothold. And the child, with their fragility and purity, often seems to be that anchor. They become the reason we wake up in the morning, the reason we go to work, the reason we don't give up. But what happens when that "reason" is no longer just a source of inspiration, but becomes the sole justification for our existence?

The child who gives meaning to a parent's life is, in fact, a child carrying an invisible burden. They feel, without being told, that they are not allowed to fail, to pull away, or to change. They feel they must be "good," "grateful," and "not disappoint." Because somewhere deep in their soul, they know that their parent's happiness depends on them. And this teaches them to live not for themselves, but for the other.

I have worked with adolescents who couldn't leave for university in another city—not because they lacked resources, but because they felt they were "abandoning their mother." With young people who didn't allow themselves to be sad, angry, or rebellious because "my mother has suffered enough; I can't give her more headaches." With children who became adults too soon because the parent needed an emotional pillar, not a son.

These children grow up with an identity confusion: "Who am I, if I exist only to give meaning to someone else's life?" They learn to define themselves through the role of the "good child," the "savior child," the "child who doesn't disappoint." But behind these masks hides a silent pain: the need to be seen, not used. To be loved, not idealized. To be free, not responsible for someone else's happiness.

This dynamic is not always conscious. The parent doesn't say, "You are the meaning of my life, so you must save me." But they convey it through gestures, through silences, through looks. Through the way they crumble when the child moves away. Through the way they make the child feel guilty for their own freedom.

And yet, the child is not the meaning of life. They are a part of it, but not its entire justification. The meaning of life needs to be constructed from within—through healing, authentic relationships, passions, and the courage to simply be. Because when the meaning of life is externalized, the child no longer has the freedom to be themselves.

For many parents, a child arrives during an existential crisis: after a breakup, a loss, a depression, or a loss of self. In that context, the child becomes "the reason I live," "my only joy," "my everything." These statements, though they seem full of gratitude, hide a dangerous projection: the child is no longer a separate being, but an extension of the wounded self. They are no longer loved for who they are, but for what they represent.

Alice Miller, in her work on childhood trauma, speaks of the "adapted child"—that child who learns to be exactly what the parent needs, giving up on themselves. It is the child who makes no noise, who doesn't disturb, who doesn't ask. It is the child who becomes the meaning of life but loses their own sense of self.

This unhealthy motivation is not an act of selfishness, but a symptom of unhealed pain. The parent is not bad; they are wounded. They are not abusive; they are lost. But that is exactly why awareness is needed—the courage to look in the mirror and admit: "I need to build a meaning for my life beyond my child."

Meaning is what transforms action into conscious choice. Without meaning, life becomes a series of automatic gestures, lacking direction. It is like setting out on a journey and being upset that we haven't arrived, only to realize we never set a destination. When we understand *why* we do something, that action gains weight, value, and motivation.

A student who understands that learning is not just an obligation, but an investment in their own freedom, will learn with greater ease. An adult who understands that exercise is not just a physical activity, but a form of self-care, will move not out of guilt, but out of respect for their own body. Meaning is not a luxury; it is a psychological necessity.

But precisely because meaning is so important, it must be chosen with discernment. Building it around a child may seem noble, but it becomes risky when that meaning is exclusive. A child cannot be the sole source of validation, motivation, and direction. Healthy meaning is plural, flexible, and internal. It feeds on relationships, passions, contribution, and personal evolution. The child can be *part* of this meaning, but they must not be its entire foundation. Otherwise, meaning becomes a burden, and the child becomes a prisoner of a mission that never belonged to them.

The Viennese psychiatrist Viktor Frankl tells us that the meaning of life cannot be imposed from the outside—it must be discovered, built, and embraced. When meaning is projected onto the child, they become a container for the parent's unfulfilled needs. And the child, unconsciously, begins to live not for themselves, but to maintain the adult's emotional balance. The implicit message becomes: "If you are well, I can breathe. If you love me, I exist."

But what happens when "meaning" grows up, finds a voice, desires, and courage? When the child becomes an adult and claims their right to autonomy, to their own path, to leaving? For the parent who has built their life around the child, this detachment can be experienced as a loss, an abandonment, a collapse. Not because the relationship is broken, but because the meaning evaporates. In the absence of an internal sense of meaning, the parent remains suspended between nostalgia and disorientation, between love and resentment. They ask themselves: "If I am no longer necessary, who am I? What is my purpose?"

This is where the need for reconstruction arises. A parent's life needs to rest on pillars that do not depend on the child's presence: on personal identity, on adult relationships, on passions, on multiple meanings. The child is not a project, but a relationship. They are not a mission, but an encounter. And when they leave, the parent must not fade away, but find themselves. They must allow themselves to be more than just a mother or a father. To be a human being. With dreams, with desires, and with paths that do not end with the child's departure, but are only just beginning.

"A child can be a light in a parent's life, but they must not be the lighthouse that guides them through the darkness."

10.1. Implications and Consequences

When a child becomes the meaning of a parent's life, the relationship is burdened with an intensity that exceeds the boundaries of healthy love. It is no longer just about care, affection, or companionship; it becomes a form of emotional dependency masked as devotion. The parent no longer lives for themselves, but through the child. And the child, instead of being encouraged to discover who they are, is taught to support, to compensate, and to never leave.

For the parent, this choice may feel lifesaving. In a moment of wandering, pain, or loss, the child becomes the anchor. They become the reason the parent continues to live, the reason they do not give up. But this motivation, if not accompanied by personal reconstruction, transforms into dependency. The parent no longer seeks multiple meanings, no longer explores, and no longer grows. They cling to the child as their sole source of validation. And when the child naturally and inevitably moves away during the process of maturation, the parent collapses. Not because the relationship is broken, but because their meaning has vanished.

For the child, the implications are profound and often invisible. They feel, from their earliest years, that they are "everything" to the parent. They feel they are not allowed to make mistakes, to rebel, or to distance themselves—that their freedom is a threat to the adult's emotional balance. Over time, the child learns to define themselves through the role of the "good child," the "savior child," or the "child who does not disappoint." But behind these masks hides a silent pain: the need to be seen for who they are, not for what they provide. The need to be loved without conditions, without missions, and without pressure.

As an adult, this child carries an identity confusion within. They do not know what it means to live for themselves, to choose themselves, or to build a life that is not based on saving others. They believe that thinking of themselves is a sign of selfishness. They enter relationships where they take on the role of supporter, pillar, or fixer. They choose professions involving helping others, not just out of vocation, but out of a deep-seated need to repeat what they were taught: "My value comes from what I provide." And when they can no longer provide, they feel useless, empty, and lost—just as their parents felt after they left home.

In this context, the parent-child relationship is marked by imbalance. It is built on dependency, not trust; on functionality, not authenticity. The parent does not see the child as a being in the making, but as a source of meaning. And the child does not feel free to be themselves, but responsible for the family's emotional stability. This relationship allows no room for vulnerability, does not encourage exploration, and does not support individuality. It is a relationship where love is conditional and freedom is negotiated.

At a social level, this dynamic perpetuates a subtle form of stagnation. The parent who lives exclusively through the child no longer contributes actively to the community, no longer explores, and no longer creates. The child, taught to be "everything" to someone, does not develop autonomy, does not take risks, and does not build a separate identity. It creates a generation of adults who do not know how to live for themselves, who confuse love with sacrifice, presence with duty, and commitment with self-abandonment.

The implications are therefore systemic. They affect the individual, the family, and the community. Most gravely, they affect the child—the one who did not choose to be there, but who will carry the entire weight of a decision made out of lack, not out of love.

10.2. Alternatives and Reflections

When a child becomes the sole meaning of a parent's life, the relationship becomes charged with an invisible but persistent tension—a pressure that can suffocate the freedom of both parties.

To break free from this dynamic and build a more balanced relationship, the parent can explore the following healthy alternatives:

- Diversifying sources of meaning. Living through a child may seem noble, but it is incomplete. A parent can rediscover personal joys—be it painting, gardening, volunteering, or simply solitary walks that nourish the soul. Meaning can be found in small but authentic things.
- Reconnecting with oneself. In the turmoil of caring for a child, a parent can forget who they were before becoming a "mother" or "father." Returning to oneself involves the courage to ask what defines them beyond their roles, what moves them, what hurts them, and what heals them.
- Redefining the parental role. Being a parent does not mean controlling; it means accompanying. It is a transition from "I know what's best for you" to "let's discover together." It is about offering space, not just protection.
- Building a rich inner life. An inner life nourished by reading, music, spirituality, or contemplation creates fertile ground for healthy relationships. When a parent has their own universe, the child is no longer the sole source of light.
- Individual or family therapy. Sometimes, wounds are too deep to be healed through introspection alone. Therapy offers a safe space to understand, to cry, to reconstruct, and to rewrite. It is a form of profound care, not only for oneself but also for the relationship with the child.

These alternatives are not magic solutions, but steps toward a relationship where love does not suffocate, but supports.

Where meaning is not imposed, but chosen. Where the child is not a substitute for the parent's voids, but a free being, accompanied with gentleness.

Reflection Questions

- What part of myself have I sacrificed in order to be "enough" as a parent?
- What scares me the most about the day my child will eventually leave?
- What makes me feel that, without my child, I no longer have value?
- What brought me joy before I became a parent, and what is stopping me from going back there?
- How can I be vulnerable in front of my child without making them responsible for my emotional state?
- What other new meanings can I identify for my life?
- What new activities can we try together as a couple?
- In what other ways can I express the concerns I have regarding my child?

Chapter 11

Unhealthy Motivation 9: The Surprise or the Unwanted Pregnancy

---

"Whether your pregnancy was meticulously planned or happened by surprise, one thing is certain: your life will never be the same again."
Catherine Jones

In this chapter, we will explore what happens when a child appears in a moment of confusion, helplessness, or lack of choice. We will look with compassion, yet with lucidity, at the implications of this unhealthy motivation. We will seek alternatives that do not deny the pain but transform it. And we will learn how to release the child from the role of a "consequence" and view them as a being with the right to be loved without conditions.

There are moments in life when decisions are not made; they simply happen. Where life is not planned but imposed by a chance occurrence, a mistake, or a night where protection was missing or ignored. An unwanted pregnancy is not just a biological reality; it is a rupture in the adult's emotional journey. It is a confrontation with one's own limits, fears, and helplessness. And in this context, the child is not a choice, but a consequence.

For some, the news of an unplanned pregnancy comes as a shock. For others, as a sentence. And in the most painful cases, as a surrender of the self. Not all parents who bring an unwanted child into the world are absent or abusive. Many of them try, strive, and adapt. But deep down, an unspoken question remains: "What would my life have been like if this child hadn't appeared?" If this question is not confronted and healed, it transforms into an invisible tension that affects the parent-child relationship and the partners' bond.

The child feels it. They feel they were not wanted. They feel their presence is tolerated, not celebrated. They feel they must compensate, behave exemplarily, and never disturb. This pressure, though subtle, becomes the foundation of an identity built on guilt. The child learns that they must earn love, that they must justify themselves, that they must be "good" to avoid being rejected.

In some cases, the parent sacrifices themselves completely, but with resentment. They give up their career, freedom, and dreams, and over time, they project onto the child the responsibility for all these sacrifices. "Because of you, I could no longer..."—an unspoken phrase, yet deeply felt. The child becomes the carrier of a burden that does not belong to them. And the relationship transforms into a field of tension rather than a space of love.

An unwanted pregnancy is not a failure; it is a reality that demands accountability. What matters is not how the story began, but how it is lived out. The parent has the responsibility to heal their resentment, to reconstruct their sense of meaning, and to learn to love out of choice, not out of obligation. The child has the right to be seen, not just tolerated. To be loved, not compensated. To be free, not conditioned.

A child who comes into the world without being wanted is not guilty. They are not responsible for the context in which they appeared. But they will feel, in every gesture, every look, and every silence, whether they are loved or merely accepted. This difference, subtle yet devastating, can shape their entire life. For the parent who did not choose but was chosen by circumstances, the true challenge is not just "to manage," but to transform resentment into accountability, frustration into meaning, and the child from a burden into an authentic relationship. It is not easy. But it is possible. And healing begins where we stop lying to ourselves and start looking with honesty.

A pregnancy is not a method of contraception. It is not a backup solution or a "fix" following a night of inattention or impulse. It is a biological and emotional reality that comes with profound responsibilities, not reversible options. Treating a pregnancy as an intermediate stage—as a "we'll see if it happens"—means ignoring the fact that what is at stake is not just one's body, but the future of a being. The child is not a mishap on the road, but a living consequence with needs, emotions, and the right to be wanted and loved.

When the news of a surprise pregnancy hits, it doesn't just come with a positive test, but with a question that changes everything: "What do we do now?" At that moment, the mother—and by extension, the couple—faces a choice with no simple answers. To keep the pregnancy means accepting a new life but also perhaps giving up on the life they imagined. To terminate the pregnancy means avoiding an unwanted reality but also opening the door to a potential trauma. Whatever the choice, it comes with an emotional cost.

If the pregnancy is carried to term, the child may unconsciously become the symbol of a sacrifice. A living memory of the road not taken. Of abandoned dreams, lost freedom, and a relationship that changed. Even if parents strive to offer love, they may project a subtle tension: "Because of you, our life doesn't look the way we hoped." If not acknowledged and healed, this dynamic can profoundly affect the parent-child relationship.

On the other hand, the choice to terminate a pregnancy is not without pain either. It is a loss. A parting from something that was only beginning to exist. It is a decision that can leave deep marks, especially in the mother's soul. Even if the choice is rational, justified, or necessary, guilt, sadness, and unanswerable questions may arise. "What if...?"—a question that can return for years.

This choice, between an unwanted life and a painful loss, is one of the hardest a human being can make. There are no perfect solutions. There is only accountability, honesty, and healing.

11.1. Implications and Consequences

An unwanted pregnancy does not end with the decision of whether or not to keep the child. It opens a long road with deep ramifications—some visible, others silent but persistent. Regardless of the choice made, the consequences seep into one's emotional life, the couple's relationship, personal identity, and the way a parent relates to themselves and to the child.

If the pregnancy is carried to term, the child becomes a permanent presence that can unconsciously reactivate the parents' resentments. Every stage—the crying of the early months, financial difficulties, the lack of personal time—can become an occasion for inner reproach: "If the child hadn't come along, I would be somewhere else now." These thoughts, even if unspoken, are felt. The child absorbs them. And the relationship is built on a fragile foundation, where love is mixed with guilt, frustration, and unfulfillment.

Within a couple, a surprise pregnancy can amplify existing tensions or create new ones. One partner may feel forced to give up their freedom, while the other may live with the feeling that they must overcompensate. Communication deteriorates, and the child becomes, unintentionally, a factor of distancing. If the relationship is not strengthened through ownership and honesty, it can turn into a space of reproaches and heavy silences.

On a personal level, the mother may experience an identity rupture. She may feel that she is no longer herself, that she has become only a "mother"—a role imposed, not chosen. Postpartum depression, anxiety, and a sense of loss of control may arise. If there is no emotional support, validation, or space for processing, these feelings can become chronic, affecting not only the relationship with the child but also with oneself.

In the case of an abortion, the emotional consequences can be just as profound as in the case of an unwanted birth. It is a choice that does not end in the doctor's office but continues in the mother's soul, in the couple's dynamics, and in the silences that follow. It can mean grief, guilt, and unanswered questions. It can mean a silent rupture that reactivates at unexpected moments: on an anniversary, at the sight of a child, or in a dream. It is a choice that demands healing, not denial.

Within the couple, the termination of a pregnancy can become a shared wound, yet one experienced differently. One partner may feel relief, the other, loss. One may want to forget, the other, to talk. This difference in emotional rhythm can generate subtle but persistent conflicts. Reproaches may appear in indirect forms: "You agreed, don't forget," "You insisted, I gave in," "You moved on, I can't." Over time, these phrases become walls between two people who no longer know how to touch each other without it hurting.

For the woman, the end of a pregnancy can bring, as previously mentioned, an identity rupture. She may feel that she has lost something she never had the chance to love. She may experience guilt in silence, especially if her partner does not validate her pain. "But it wasn't the right time; we did what we had to do"—a phrase that, though logical, can sound like an invalidation of her experience. And if the woman has no space to cry, to ask questions, or to doubt, the pain closes inside her and turns into isolation.

The couple's relationship may suffer a crack that is difficult to repair. Intimacy cools. Communication becomes defensive. Each partner begins to withdraw into their own emotional universe, and the child who was not brought into the world remains like a ghost between them—an invisible but felt presence. If this wound is not processed together, with honesty and empathy, it can lead to a definitive break. Not because love has vanished, but because the pain was ignored.

During this period, when the couple or one of the partners decides to terminate a pregnancy, a subtle form of denial of suffering may emerge. Things are said like, "We are fine," "It was the right decision," or "Life goes on." But beneath these statements lies an unspoken pain, a pain that has not been processed. Denial becomes a defense mechanism, a form of emotional survival. However, what is not felt does not disappear; it only transforms.

This denial can create fertile ground for the emergence of compensatory behaviors. Some take refuge in work, others in alcohol, compulsive consumption, or the avoidance of any form of intimacy. In some cases, the temptation of infidelity arises, especially on the part of the man, who may feel he no longer recognizes the woman beside him. Perhaps he is tired of seeing her always sad, crying, or withdrawn. Perhaps he does not know how to help her and, instead of staying, he escapes. Not out of a lack of love, but out of helplessness.

Infidelity, in this context, is not just a betrayal but also an expression of an unprocessed rupture. It is a flight from pain, an attempt to rediscover something that seems lost: vitality, desire, normalcy. But this flight does not heal; it only deepens the distance. And the woman, already made fragile by the loss, may feel she is being abandoned at her most vulnerable moment. A spiral of guilt, shame, and isolation can set in.

If these dynamics are not recognized and addressed with honesty, the couple risks falling apart—not for lack of love, but from an inability to navigate the pain together. The choice to terminate a pregnancy is not just a medical decision; it is a profound emotional experience that requires space, time, and support. Without these, the pain turns into distance, and the distance into a rupture.

For the child who comes into the world without being wanted, existence can become a silent struggle for validation. Although the parent may try to compensate, the child senses—through looks, tone, and gestures—that their presence is not celebrated, but tolerated. This subtle rejection transforms into anxiety, self-shame, and the conviction that they must earn love, rather than receiving it unconditionally. The child learns to adapt, to not be a bother, to be "good," but inside they feel invisible, unimportant, and guilty for their very existence.

In future relationships, this child—now an adult—may face major difficulties in connecting authentically. They may avoid intimacy out of fear of being rejected again. They might choose emotionally unavailable partners, unconsciously recreating the cold dynamic they had with their parent. Alternatively, they may become dependent on validation, always searching for a love that confirms their right to exist. The relationship with the parent remains marked by a coldness that is difficult to define. And even in adulthood, the child may carry the unspoken question in their soul: "If you didn't want me, why did you bring me into the world?"

11.2. Alternatives and Reflections

A surprise pregnancy does not have to become a trauma; instead, it can be transformed into a moment of maturation, reconnection, and conscious choice. It is a situation that demands presence, not impulse. Clarity, not denial. And, above all, support, so that the decision made is owned, rather than dictated by fear or pressure.

To navigate this period with responsibility and balance, the couple can explore the following healthy alternatives:

- Couple's psychotherapy or psychological counseling. An unexpected pregnancy can amplify tensions, fears, or differences in vision. Psychotherapy provides a safe framework where partners can explore what they feel, what they want, and what scares them, without judgment. It is a process that fosters authentic communication, empathy, and the making of an informed, committed decision. It is not about "saving the relationship," but about understanding if and how it can continue in a healthy way.

- Prevention and psychoeducation. Ideally, discussions about children, contraception, and shared values should take place before a pregnancy occurs. However, even after the fact, psychoeducation helps in understanding options, clarifying myths, and reducing anxiety. It is a form of relational hygiene, as important as fidelity or mutual respect. Sexual education, open communication within the couple, and access to contraceptive methods are essential pillars for avoiding painful decisions.
- Active and responsible protection. The consistent and correct use of contraceptive methods is not just a technical choice, but also an act of care for oneself and for the other. Choosing the right method involves communication, information, and respect for each person's body and rhythm. Constant protection does not mean fear of pregnancy, but rather maturity in managing sexuality.
- Identifying concrete solutions for reconfiguring life. If the decision is to keep the pregnancy, the couple can begin to plan realistically: how responsibilities will be shared, what external support exists, and what lifestyle adjustments are necessary to ensure proper preparation. The child should not be an obstacle, but a challenge that can be integrated with lucidity.
- External support (familial, community, professional). Sometimes, the couple does not have to decide alone. Asking for help from family, friends, doctors, or therapists is

not a weakness, but a sign of wisdom. Support can be emotional, logistical, or financial. The important thing is that the decision is not made in isolation, but with access to real resources.

Reflection Questions:

- What do I truly feel about this pregnancy, beyond what I "should" feel?
- What fears are preventing me from seeing this situation clearly?
- What does a committed, conscious choice mean to me?
- What support do I need right now (emotional, informational, relational)?
- How do I ask for this support?
- How would I like to receive this support?
- How can I transform this experience into a moment of maturation, rather than a rupture?
- What do I want to learn from this situation about myself, my relationship, and the future?
- What is preventing me from becoming responsible for a new life?
- What is preventing me from being cautious in a situation where I am not yet ready to become a parent?

Chapter 12

Unhealthy Motivation 10: Because that is how it must be

„Social norms can be guides, but they must not be chains."

Esther Perel

There are decisions that are not born out of desire, but out of conformity. Not from choice, but from obedience to a norm transmitted, sometimes, without words. "Because that's what you must do" is a phrase that carries the weight of a generation, of a culture, of a collective silence. It is the voice of the mother who had no options, of the grandmother who was never asked, of a society that confused motherhood with duty. But what happens when this motivation becomes the only thread supporting a decision as profound as continuing a pregnancy?

There are decisions born not from the heart, but from the norm. From a "this is how it's done" passed down through generations, from judging glances and heavy silences. Carrying a pregnancy to term "because you must" is not a choice; it is surrender. It is a renunciation of the self in favor of an abstract idea of "correctness." But who decides what is correct? Naturally, everyone should decide for themselves what is right.

For many women, this motivation does not appear as a loud voice, but as a constant, insinuating whisper accompanying every stage of life. It is the voice of the mother saying, "it's not right to give up," perhaps the voice of the priest uttering, "a child is a gift," or the voice of society looking at you with suspicion if you do not conform. It is the voice that doesn't ask how you feel, but what is required. In the face of this voice, many women shut down their own questions, their own fears, their own desires. They submit. They conform. They lose themselves.

Yes, a child is a gift, a miracle, life itself. But what if you are not ready to receive this gift? It is as if you live in a tiny studio apartment and your friends decide to gift you a Labrador. You didn't ask for it, you weren't consulted, you didn't want it. Others decided for you.

"Because that's what you must do" is not a motivation; it is a constraint. It is not a choice, but an avoidance of conflict. It is not accountability, but a flight from judgment. It is a form of obedience hiding behind the mask of maturity. But real maturity does not mean doing what is expected of you. It means knowing what you want, understanding what you can handle, and choosing what you feel. It means taking responsibility for the consequences of a decision that comes from within you, not from others.

This motivation is all the more dangerous because it appears "correct." It seems moral. It looks responsible. But in reality, it can lead to profound ruptures: in the relationship with oneself, with the partner, and with the child. A woman who carries a pregnancy to term only because "that's what you must do" may end up living with resentment, repressed anger, and the haunting feeling that her life no longer belongs to her. She may feel captive in a role she did not choose, but merely accepted out of fear. This captivity isn't always visible on the surface; it hides in chronic fatigue, constant irritability, a lack of joy, and long silences that no longer ask for anything.

Behind "because you must" lies an entire culture of silence. A culture that does not encourage the question "How do I feel?" but instead imposes the answer "This is what is done." It is a culture that values sacrifice but ignores suffering; one that idealizes motherhood but never speaks of ambivalence, fear, or the loss of identity. It pressures women to be mothers without ever asking if they want to, if they can, or if they are ready. In this environment, "because you must" becomes a phrase that justifies everything: abandoning dreams, staying in toxic relationships, or an uncommitted motherhood.

Yet, there is a moment when this phrase begins to crack. It might be a sleepless night overwhelmed by thoughts. It might be a conversation with a friend who asks, sincerely, "What do *you* want?" It might be a therapy session where, for the first time, she allows herself to say, "I don't know if I want this." It might be a moment of lucidity when she realizes her life doesn't have to follow a script written by others. And then, "because you must" begins to transform. It becomes "because I choose." It becomes "because I feel." It becomes "because I understand."

This transformation is not easy. It is painful, filled with doubt, fear, and guilt. But it is authentic. It is alive. It is liberating. Because at that moment, the woman no longer lives according to what is expected of her, but according to who she truly is. Perhaps the choice will still be to keep the pregnancy—but it will be a choice, not an obligation. Not a surrender, not a replica of a social norm.

"Because that's what you must do" is a phrase that can destroy lives if left unquestioned. But if viewed with honesty, courage, and lucidity, it can become the beginning of an inner revolution. It can be the moment a woman reclaims her voice, her body, and her life.

I remember a client who was preparing for her wedding without feeling any real desire to get married. She was lucid, conscious, and even courageous in the way she questioned herself. One evening, a few days before the ceremony, she told her grandmother: "I'm not in love with him. I don't feel he's the person I want to spend my life with." Her grandmother smiled gently, almost as an accomplice, and replied: "That's normal. You'll see, you'll get used to it."

That reply, spoken with a calmness that seemed to belong to another era, was a capsule of emotional history. Within it was hidden an entire transgenerational heritage—a culture of resignation, of forced adaptation, of love as a habit rather than a choice. The grandmother wasn't being cynical or cold; she was simply the carrier of a survival logic passed down by women who never had the luxury of asking what they felt. Women who were taught that love comes later, that happiness is built on acceptance rather than compatibility. That "getting used to it" is enough.

This inheritance is not transmitted through words alone, but through gestures, silences, glances, and the unsaid. It lives in the way girls are taught not to be "picky," not to "ruin a good thing," and not to "disappoint the family." It is in the way mothers urge their daughters to accept, to endure, and to refrain from asking uncomfortable questions. It is in the way love becomes a duty rather than a choice. And when a woman faces an unexpected pregnancy, this inheritance can become the dominant voice—overshadowing what she feels with "what is done," and replacing what she wants with "what must be."

But what happens when this voice is no longer enough? When a woman begins to feel that she does not want to "get used to it," but to choose? When she realizes that life is not a ritual of adaptation, but a space for creation? That is when the rupture begins. It is not a rupture with the grandmother, but with the idea that she must live the same way. A break from the notion that love is learned rather than felt, and that motherhood is a duty rather than a calling.

That client did not run away from the wedding. But she began to ask questions. She began to wonder what a relationship meant to her, what presence meant, and what choice meant. In that process, she began to detach herself from the heritage that was pushing her toward "because you must." She did so not with rebellion, but with lucidity; not with hatred, but with gratitude and discernment.

Transgenerational inheritance should not be denied. It needs to be known, explored, and understood. It needs to be placed under a magnifying glass. The moment we know our history, we can choose: what we keep, what we leave behind, and what we transform. Only then can we live a life that is not a copy, but a creation. Only then can we truly say, "I do not have to; I choose to."

Perhaps we don't have to. Perhaps it is time to choose.

12.1. Implications and Consequences

When a woman keeps a pregnancy only because "that is how it must be," the consequences are not just external; they infiltrate the most intimate layers of her being. On the surface, everything may seem fine: a relationship that continues, a family that approves, a society that validates her. But inside, a subtle rupture can set in—a dissonance between what she experiences and what she feels. And this dissonance does not manifest immediately; it accumulates over time, like water silently eroding stone.

One of the most frequent implications is the loss of contact with oneself. The woman begins to live according to an imposed script, rather than an authentic choice. She finds herself in a life that does not truly belong to her, where every day is an adaptation rather than an affirmation. This loss of self is not seen in grand gestures, but in details: in the way she remains silent when she would like to speak, in the way she smiles when she would like to run away, in the way she asks herself, in solitude, "what if...?"

The consequences also extend to the couple's relationship. If the decision to keep the child was not a shared, committed one, discussed in depth, tensions can arise that are difficult to manage. The partners may become strangers, united only by responsibility, not by love. Communication can transform into an exchange of tasks, not emotions. And the child, though innocent, can become the symbol of a rupture, of an unowned choice, of a life lived "because that is how it must be."

Furthermore, motherhood experienced out of obligation can also affect the relationship with the child. Not in an obvious way, not through violent gestures, but in the absence of authentic joy, in the difficulty of creating a deep bond, in the feeling that something is missing. The child senses this, even if they do not understand it. They sense when the mother is not truly present, when love is mechanical, when the smile is tired. And this void can be passed on like an emotional inheritance—a silent lesson on how life is lived: with resignation, not with choice.

In the long run, the woman may come to wonder if her life is truly her own. She may feel that she was pushed into a role that does not suit her, that she gave up on dreams, freedom, and authenticity. She may live with the feeling that she has been loyal to everyone except herself. And this misplaced loyalty can become the source of a diffuse sadness, a chronic fatigue, a need for escape that has no form, but has weight.

The implications are not only psychological but also existential. Because a decision made out of "must" is not just a wrong choice; it is a loss of meaning. And meaning, once lost, is not easily recovered. It requires courage, introspection, support, and, above all, the permission to ask uncomfortable questions. To say, "I no longer want to live like this." To acknowledge that "how it must be" is not enough. That life deserves more than a line passed down from generation to generation. It deserves truth. It deserves freedom. It deserves choice.

A child does not demand perfection. They do not ask for parents who know everything, who never make mistakes, or who never tire. A child asks for presence. They ask for warmth. They ask to be seen, heard, and felt. They ask for love that is not negotiated, acceptance that is not conditioned, and validation that is not delayed. And when a mother is not truly there—not physically, but emotionally—the child senses it. They sense it in the vacant gaze, in the hurried touch, in the mechanical response. They sense they are unwanted, even if it is never said. They sense they are tolerated, not loved. They sense they are an obligation, not a choice.

This coldness does not always manifest as direct rejection. Sometimes, it is a subtle but constant distance. The mother fulfills her role—she feeds, washes, organizes—but she is absent from the affective space. And the child, in the absence of this connection, begins to wonder what is wrong with them. Why are they not enough? Why are they not loved? Why are they not seen?

The need for love, acceptance, and validation is fundamental. It is not a whim; it is not a bonus; it is the child's emotional oxygen. Without it, a void sets in. A void that can transform into anxiety, insecurity, and self-doubt. A void that can later become a desperate need for approval, a dependency on relationships, or an inability to feel whole without external confirmation.

And it all starts with that "because that is how it must be." From motherhood lived as a duty, not a choice. From a presence that is not accompanied by love. From a mother who was never asked how she feels and who, in turn, does not ask how the child feels. Thus, a cold lineage is perpetuated—a genealogy of distance, a legacy of unfulfilled need.

But this lineage can be interrupted. It can be questioned. It can be healed. The moment a mother acknowledges her own rupture, her own lack of ownership, her own pain, she can begin to reconnect. Not perfectly, not suddenly, but honestly. She can begin to see the child not as a consequence, but as a being. Not as an obligation, but as a relationship. Not as a replica of a norm, but as an opportunity to love differently than she was loved.

A child does not need an ideal mother. They need a present mother. A mother who says, "I see you," "I hear you," "I feel you." A mother who, even if she did not initially choose with her heart, chooses now with her conscience. She chooses to be there. She chooses to love. She chooses to repair.

Because love is not learned from "how it must be." It is learned from "how I feel." And sometimes, it takes only one authentic gesture for a child to begin believing they are worthy of love. And that gesture can be the beginning of a relationship that no longer repeats the past, but transforms it.

There is a line passed down from mother to mother like a magic promise: "Don't worry, you'll see how everything changes once you hold the baby in your arms." It is spoken with conviction, with a smile, with a certainty that seems to leave no room for doubt. It is as if maternal instinct should appear instantaneously, like a revelation—a miraculous transformation that erases all fears, all doubts, and all ambivalence. Many future mothers cling to this promise. They hope that, in that moment, everything will fall into place. That they will feel the love, the connection, the certainty. That they will finally become "real mothers."

But what happens when this miracle doesn't appear? What happens when, instead of a revelation, comes confusion? When, instead of instant love, there is a sense of emptiness, of not belonging, of alienation? What happens when a woman holds her child and feels nothing? Or feels fear? Or feels that she isn't ready? That it isn't her? That she isn't really there?

This disappointment can be devastating. It is not just a lack of emotion; it is a profound discrepancy between expectation and reality. The woman feels broken. She feels guilty. She wonders what is wrong with her. Why doesn't she feel what she "should" feel? Why hasn't she transformed, just as she was told she would? And instead of being encouraged to speak about this, she is often met with misunderstanding, judgment, or advice that reduces her to silence: "It's normal, it will pass," "All mothers go through this," "Stop thinking such nonsense."

But it isn't normal. It isn't easy. And it doesn't pass without support. For some women, this period can spiral into postpartum depression. Into anxiety. Into rejection of the child. Into anger toward the partner—especially if he wanted the child more, if he seems happy, if he doesn't understand what is happening. The woman feels alone in an experience that was meant to be shared. She feels betrayed by her own body, by her own emotions, and by the promise that went unfulfilled.

It all starts with that "you'll see." With the idea that motherhood is automatic, that maternal love is guaranteed, and that instinct appears like a reflex. But the reality is far more complex. Motherhood is not a reflex; it is a relationship. Maternal love is not a given; it is a process. Instinct is not universal; it is influenced by context, personal history, emotional readiness, and support. When these conditions are missing, it is only natural for a woman not to feel what she "should." Not because she is broken, but because she is human.

This story must be told. It must be validated. It must be understood. Because without it, women continue to live in silence, guilt, and shame. They continue to believe they are alone, that they are wrong, that they are not "real mothers." But the truth is that motherhood is not measured by instinct, but by presence. Not by magic, but by emotional labor. Not by automatism, but by choice.

Perhaps, instead of telling future mothers, "Don't worry, you'll see," it would be more honest to ask them: "What are you feeling right now?", "What scares you?", "What do you need to feel ready?". Perhaps, instead of promises, we should offer space. Space for doubt, for fear, for ambivalence. Space for the truth. Because only there, in that space, can love truly emerge—not as a reflex, but as a choice. Not as magic, but as an authentic encounter between mother and child.

I have often heard the phrase, "You're almost out" or "You're almost free" (*mai ai puțin și scapi*). Spoken with a complicit smile in a park or a supermarket line, it seems harmless at first glance. It usually happens when a mother asks a pregnant woman how far along she is. But if we look at it closely, with lucidity, it reveals a much deeper reality: a distorted perception of motherhood, a normalization of discomfort, and a lack of space for the authentic experience of those nine months.

When you use the verb "to escape" or "to get out of," you are generally referring to something you dislike, something that constrains you, something you want to end. It is a word that carries the idea of evasion, of liberation from an unwanted state. When applied to pregnancy, you convey—consciously or not—that this period is a punishment, a prison, a difficult stage to be endured rather than lived. It is as if the pregnant woman were a prisoner in her own body, and birth were the moment the cell door finally opens.

This mindset not only trivializes the complexity of pregnancy but also loads it with negativity. A pregnant woman, especially if it is her first experience, may internalize this idea. She may begin to believe that she must simply bear it, endure it, and rush toward the finish line. She may feel she isn't allowed to enjoy, to connect, or to experience each stage with meaning. Even worse, she may hope that once the birth is over, everything will be resolved—that she will instantly feel love, instinct, and certainty. But if she is not emotionally prepared, if she hasn't been encouraged to connect with herself, her body, and her child, she may face a profound disappointment. She may feel that she didn't "escape," but rather entered another stage just as overwhelming, yet without the promise of liberation.

This phrase, repeated in social contexts, becomes a form of validating a culture of accepted discomfort. A culture where women are not encouraged to ask what they feel, but to conform. Not to complain. Not to doubt. Not to stop. To "escape." But motherhood is not something to escape from. It is something to be lived, felt, and understood. It is an experience that demands presence, not haste; connection, not evasion.

Perhaps it is time to change this narrative. To replace it with "You're almost ready for something new," "You're almost at the point where you will discover yourself differently," or "You're almost there to feel what it means to be truly present." Perhaps it is time to talk about pregnancy not as a difficult phase, but as an inner journey. Not as a punishment, but as a transformation. Not as something to be endured, but as something that can be chosen, lived, and integrated.

Because a pregnant woman is not a prisoner. She is a being in the making. And she deserves to be accompanied with gentleness, not clichés. With truth, not automatism. With respect, not haste.

12.2. Alternatives and Reflections

In many social contexts, the decision to have children seems to follow a predefined, almost automatic path: you get married, you buy a house, you have a child. It is not necessarily a choice, but a checked box, a cultural duty, a norm passed down from generation to generation. "This is how it's done." "That's what you must do." But what happens when this decision does not come from a space of authentic desire, but from pressure, conformity, or the fear of judgment? What kind of relationship is built with the child, with oneself, and with parenthood, when the starting point is not freedom, but obligation?

Having a child should not be a reaction to the expectations of others, but a conscious, personal, and accountable choice.

Here are some healthy alternatives for those who feel they "must" have children but are not sure if this desire truly belongs to them:

- Giving myself time to discover what motherhood means to me. In a hurried society where the "biological clock" is invoked like a sword over one's head, the idea of taking your time might seem like a luxury. In reality, it is a necessity. Becoming a mother is not a decision to be made between two meetings or based on what your friends are doing. It is a choice that demands introspection, space, and silence. It might take years to truly feel if motherhood is part of your personal path. And that is perfectly okay. Time is not an enemy; it is an ally of authentic choices.
- Asking myself if the desire comes from within or from the outside. It is easy to mistake the inner voice for the echo of others. "I'd like to have a child" can sometimes be a learned line rather than a felt reality. Sincerely questioning the source of this desire is an act of courage. It may stem from family pressure, the fear of loneliness, or comparison with others.

Or, it may come from a profound space—an inner calling. Only you can tell the difference.

- Allowing myself not to want children without feeling guilty. In a culture that glorifies motherhood as the ultimate fulfillment, the absence of a desire for children is often viewed as an anomaly. It is not. It is a valid, mature, and deep choice. Not wanting children does not mean you are selfish, cold, or incomplete. It means you know your limits, your needs, and your path. Saying "no" to a norm is sometimes the most profound "yes" you can say to your own life.
- Considering the kind of life I want to build. Children are not a guarantee of happiness; they are a possible part of a whole. Asking yourself what kind of life you want—what rhythm, what freedoms, what types of relationships—helps you see if motherhood fits into that picture. Perhaps you want a nomadic life, perhaps you want to dedicate yourself to a cause, or perhaps you want to explore other forms of creation. Life is not a recipe; it is a personal composition.
- Talking to people who have chosen differently. Exposure to a diversity of choices opens our minds. You may have friends who are fulfilled as parents, or you may know women who chose not to have children and live with deep meaning. Listening to others' stories helps clarify your own—not to copy them, but to understand. Dialogue is not contamination; it is clarification.
- Allowing myself to change my mind over time. What you feel now is not a life sentence. Perhaps today you don't want children, but in five years you will feel differently. Or vice versa. Allowing yourself to evolve and revisit decisions is a

sign of maturity, not instability. Life is fluid, and you are allowed to be fluid as well. Constancy is not rigidity; it is fidelity to the self, even as the self changes.

- Psychotherapy as a space for clarity and conscious choice. Psychotherapy offers a safe framework where a woman can explore, without haste or judgment, what motherhood means to her. Beyond the social noise and family expectations, there is an inner voice that deserves to be heard. In the therapist's office, questions can be spoken without fear: *Do I truly want a child? Or do I feel that I must?* Therapy differentiates desires from fears and needs from loyalties, allowing choices to become freer and more accountable.
- Transgenerational legacies: What we carry forward and what we leave behind. Every woman carries a history that did not begin with her: stories, patterns, and emotions passed down through generations. Sometimes, the desire for a child comes from an invisible loyalty to a mother, a grandmother, or the female line of the family. Other times, the fear of repeating their suffering blocks authentic desire. Exploring these legacies—what was transmitted, what heals, and what hurts—is an essential step. Becoming a mother means deciding which part of your history you want to carry forward and which part you choose, with love, to stop.

Reflection Questions:

- What do I feel when I truly think about the idea of having a child?
- If no one ever asked me "When are you having a baby?", what would I choose for myself?

- What does a "fulfilled life" mean to me, and where does motherhood fit within it?
- Which part of me wants a child: my body, my soul, my mind—or is it just my mother's voice in my head?
- What would it be like to live without following the "normal" path? What freedom would that bring me?
- What messages about motherhood did I receive during my own childhood?
- Which patterns from my family do I want to keep? Which do I want to transform?
- If I were completely free from the expectations of others, what would I choose?
- Which part of me fears that I won't be "enough" if I don't become a mother?
- Which part of me fears that I won't be "enough" if I *do* become a mother?

Chapter 13

I will have a child when I will have one....

„Control is the substitute we choose when we lack trust."

Dr. Gabor Maté

There is a phrase that frequently appears in conversations about parenthood: "I will have a child when I have…", followed by a list of conditions, some pragmatic, others idealized. *When I have money. When I have a stable relationship. When I have time. When I have healed. When I am less tired. When I am less selfish. When I am more myself.*

These conditions may seem natural, even responsible. And sometimes, they are. But often, they hide a subtle flight from the real question: "What makes me believe I must be someone other than who I am to become a parent?" Behind these "when I have..." statements lies a desire for control, security, and perfection. It is the illusion that there is an ideal moment—a fixed point in time where all the pieces align and life becomes smooth enough to add a child to the landscape.

But life does not work that way. It rarely offers certainties. And it never guarantees that once you have checked every box, you are truly ready. Parenthood is not a reward for reaching a threshold; it is a choice that demands presence, not perfection.

The truth is that many people have children in moments of vulnerability, confusion, or impulse. Others, conversely, postpone indefinitely, waiting for that "when I have..." that never comes. Between these two extremes lies a zone of lucidity: the understanding that you don't need to be *complete*, but *conscious*. You don't need to have everything; you need to be willing to offer what you have with authenticity.

Having a child does not mean having everything under control. It means being willing to lose control, to learn, to make mistakes, and to rebuild yourself. It means being there, even when you don't know what you're doing. It means being there, not because you checked all the boxes, but because you chose to be present.

Perhaps "I will have a child when..." is not always a rational choice, but an attempt to negotiate with one's own fears. Sometimes, the body feels before the mind understands. Other times, the mind constructs scenarios that do not align with deep desire. In the silence between these two voices—the inner one and the social one—a confusion is born: *Do I truly want a child, or do I just think I should want one?* In a world that teaches us to be "prepared" for everything, it is hard to accept that some choices do not come from logic, but from an inner trembling that cannot be explained, only listened to.

There is a popular saying that "everything happens in its own time." It is an expression that carries simple wisdom but also a subtle limitation. For some, it becomes a compass—a form of trust that life has its own rhythms and nothing should be forced.

For others, however, it can become an obstacle, a justification for repeated delays, or a pressure to fit into an "ideal time" that does not exist. Of course, it should not be taken literally. Life always offers space for reinvention, for late choices, for paths resumed. Becoming a parent later is not impossible, but it can be different. It might be a bit harder or easier; it depends. As time passes, patience may erode, energy fragments, and attention is divided among more responsibilities. This is not a rule, but a reality worth looking at with honesty. It doesn't mean it is "too late," but it requires more awareness, more commitment, and more presence.

This postponement—as if bringing a child into the world must follow an exhaustive checklist of career stability, a purchased home, a perfect relationship, emotional balance, and checked-off travel goals—can become a major source of anxiety. Not only because we feel pressured to hit these milestones, but because, over time, they transform into a psychological threshold that is increasingly difficult to cross. Without realizing it, this inner tension can even affect the body. Fertility issues do not arise solely from medical causes; they can stem from chronic stress, the fear of failure, and the persistent feeling that "we are not yet prepared enough." The paradox is that in our attempt to create "ideal" conditions, we may end up distancing ourselves from the very possibility of becoming parents. Perhaps we need to rethink this list—not as a set of rigid requirements, but as a flexible map that can be adapted, rewritten, and lived imperfectly.

A child—the future child—does not come with a predefined set of conditions. It isn't as if they say: "I won't be born if my mother doesn't have a stable job," or "I won't come into the world if my father doesn't hold an important leadership position." A child does not refuse existence because their parents drive a $30,000 car instead of a $100,000 one. They do not stop at the border between a 9-square-meter room and a 20-square-meter one. Life does not operate on criteria of luxury or social validation. It slips through, it is born, it happens—sometimes in the most modest of conditions, but with a love that cannot be measured in square meters or salaries. Perhaps we need to remind ourselves that a child does not ask for perfection; they ask for presence. They don't ask for status; they ask for emotional safety. They don't demand the checking of a list; they demand the availability to be there with all that we are, not with all that we think we *should* be.

Perhaps this idea of "I will have a child when..." comes, paradoxically, at a time when our patience is nearly at zero—when we are exhausted by expectations, pressures, and comparisons. In such a state, instead of being a conscious choice, parenthood risks becoming a burden. Not because we don't want the child, but because we are tired of fighting against time, exhaustion, and our own limits. In a context where everything is demanded immediately, where performance is constant and validation is external, the idea of caring for another human being, day and night, can feel overwhelming. And yet, this might be the key: to ask ourselves not just *when* we want to become parents, but *how* we want to be in that role. With what kind of presence, what kind of availability, and what kind of patience?

"I will have a child when I have..."—a phrasing that can hide a profound need for control behind the mask of responsibility. It is a subtle avoidance, an unspoken fear, a desire to reduce the unknown to a checklist. It is natural to want stability, safety, and predictability. But life doesn't always work according to the plan. What happens when, despite all the calculations, you become pregnant before the list is complete? When the room isn't ready, the job isn't secure, the relationship isn't "perfect"? It can be a moment of confusion, of internal renegotiation, of re-evaluating priorities. It can be hard and unexpected, but not necessarily wrong. Sometimes, it is precisely these moments that challenge us to look honestly at what truly matters and to discover that we can build as we go—not just after everything seems "ready."

Perhaps the question should not be "When will I have a child?", but "How will I *be* when I have a child?". Or, more deeply: "Who am I right now, and what kind of parent would I be if I chose to become one?"

Reflection Questions:

- What conditions have I set, consciously or unconsciously, before becoming a parent?
- Are these conditions realistic or idealized? Do they serve me, or do they block me?
- What fears are hidden behind these conditions?
- What does "being ready" actually mean to me?
- How can I be an authentic parent even without being "ready" in an absolute sense?
- What is it that prevents me from postponing the role of a parent?
- What part of me fears being lost once a child arrives?
- What image do I have of the "ideal parent," and where does this image come from?
- What is my relationship with the idea of control, and how does it influence my decision to become a parent?

- What kind of emotional heritage do I carry, and how might it influence the way I parent?
- What makes me believe I need to be "different" than I am now to be enough?
- What expectations do I have of my child before they even exist?
- What part of me feels unseen or unvalidated and is seeking confirmation through parenthood?
- What does "being safe" mean to me, and how is this need linked to the decision to have a child?
- What would my child tell me, if they could, about what they truly need from me?
- What am I afraid to lose if I become a parent—and what am I afraid I will never gain?

Chapter 14

The Decision Not to Have Children

„Being a woman does not automatically mean being a mother. Being whole means being faithful to your own choice."

Esther Perel

There are moments when the silence of personal choice collides with the noise of social expectations. The decision not to have children is not an absence, but a profound presence of self-awareness. It is a choice that is not made in a single day, but one that ripens over time—through inner conversations and questions that do not always have clear answers. Sometimes it stems from a solid trust in one's own path; other times, from a lucid fear that motherhood might mean the loss of the self.

For some women, this choice is a form of freedom. The freedom to live a life without sharing it with a permanent responsibility. The freedom to dedicate themselves to other forms of creation, contribution, and love. For others, it is a form of protection—against their own wounds, against a world they cannot guarantee is safe, or against a future they cannot promise.

But behind this decision, there is often a silent struggle. A struggle with the questions that come from the outside: "Won't you regret it?", "Don't you feel incomplete?", "What is the point of life without children?" These are questions that do not seek understanding, but confirmation—confirmation of a norm stating that a woman only finds fulfillment through motherhood. Or they seek to judge.

Yet, there are women who feel whole without having given birth. Women who love, create, nurture, and build without being mothers. They are not fleeing from responsibility; they are redirecting it. They are not refusing life; they are choosing it in a different form.

This choice is not a manifesto against motherhood, but a plea for the diversity of paths. It is an invitation to respect and to silence—the silence in which a woman can hear her own voice without the echo of the world.

Perhaps not everyone will understand. Perhaps some relationships will change, and some glances will grow heavy. But in the midst of this friction, one certainty remains: a life lived in harmony with oneself is more valuable than a life lived in accordance with others under constant pressure.

I leave here the words of a client who said NO to motherhood:

"For me, this choice was not an act of rebellion, but a form of sincerity. I didn't feel the calling; I didn't feel that visceral desire to be a mother. More than that, I felt that my life could be full, rounded, and valuable even if it didn't include a child. It took courage to admit this—not to the world, but to myself. Because within me lived the voices of my mother, my grandmother, and my friends who held their children to their chests with a light in their eyes that I simply couldn't understand.

I have been asked countless times: 'But aren't you afraid you'll regret it?' And yes, I was. Regret is a ghost that haunts any definitive choice. But I learned that the fear of regret is not a sufficient reason to do something you don't feel. Regret cannot be prevented; it can only be owned.

I have been called selfish, as if having children were an act of absolute altruism. But I have also seen mothers who projected their frustrations onto their children, who demanded gratitude, who parented out of a need for validation rather than love. Selfishness is not about the choice itself; it's about the motivation behind it.

I have been asked if I don't feel incomplete—as if the womb were the center of my being. But I felt complete in the moments I wrote, in the moments I loved, in the moments I learned, and in the moments I was present in the lives of others without being their mother.

I have been looked at with pity, as if my life were a secondary option, a Plan B. But I didn't feel a lack; I felt space. Space for myself, for silence, for exploration, and for relationships that are not defined by sacrifice.

And yet, it is not an easy choice. Not because it is hard in itself, but because it is hard to maintain it in front of a world that interprets it as an anomaly. It's hard to stay silent when others want to convince you. It's hard not to doubt yourself when everyone else seems to know what's better for you than you do.

But in the midst of these tensions, I discovered something essential: a life lived in harmony with oneself is more valuable than a life lived in accordance with others. Motherhood is not an obligation, but a possibility. And saying 'no' to a possibility does not mean saying ‘no’ to life; it means saying ‘yes’ to another form of existence.

I don’t have children. And I am no less a woman. I am no less loving. I am no less whole. I am simply different.”

Women are not the only ones confronted with the question, “When will you have a child?” Men hear it too—perhaps less often, but with the same subtle pressure. In a world where masculinity is frequently conflated with virility and the capacity to “carry on the family name,” a man’s decision not to become a father can seem like a rupture of tradition, a form of denial. Yet, for some, it is a conscious and profound choice that stems not from a lack, but from lucidity.

“I don’t want to have children just because ‘that’s what people do,’” a man once told me, carrying his choice with a rare sense of calm. “I don’t feel the need to leave something behind. I don’t believe my legacy has to be biological. I prefer to leave behind ideas, gestures, and relationships that actually meant something.”

His voice wasn’t defensive; it was clear. He wasn’t speaking from fear, but from a mature understanding of what responsibility truly entails. For him, being a father wasn’t a mandatory step in personal growth, but a possibility that simply didn’t fit. He didn’t feel the calling; he didn’t feel the need to project himself into another body. Above all, he refused to become a father out of loyalty to a lineage that didn’t represent him.

“People told me I’d regret it. Maybe. But I don’t want to live with the regret of bringing a child into this world just because I had to. The regret of being absent, of being unprepared, of being a half-hearted father.”

This voice deserves to be heard. Because men, too, have the right to choose. They, too, can feel that their lives are whole without children. They, too, can refuse to become parents.

The decision not to have children, whether made by a woman or a man, is not an escape; it is a positioning. It is not a lack, but a profound form of presence. It is not a rupture, but a choice to build differently.

Some people choose not to become parents not out of a lack of love, but out of a deep respect for the complexity of life. These are women and men who have learned to look at their limits with honesty—viewing them not as a source of shame, but as a sign of maturity. They don't run from responsibility; they understand it so well that they know they cannot pass it on unless they have first learned to carry it for themselves. They are aware of their desires and their need for authenticity, knowing that their choices must belong entirely to them—uncontaminated by pressures, traditions, or expectations that do not reflect who they are.

Often, they carry heavy legacies: a painful childhood, a toxic relationship with parents, perhaps a hereditary illness that changed their perspective on fragility. They refuse to pass on what has not yet been healed. They understand that this piece of their life's puzzle is still aching, still struggling between acceptance and rebellion, and that bringing a new life into the middle of this unrest would be an injustice. They don't feel ready to be parents because they are still learning how to parent their own inner child.

They know that responsibility isn't measured by desire, but by the capacity to sustain, to be present, and to provide stability. Precisely because they cannot guarantee these things, they choose not to promise what they cannot fulfill. It is a painful choice at times, but a deeply ethical one. It is a form of love that goes unseen, but protects. It is a testament to lucidity in a world that confuses maturity with conformity.

It is as if you live in a city where everyone dreams of climbing a great tower. From a young age, we are told that at the top, we will find light, meaning, and fulfillment. We are shown photos of the view; we are told of the thin air and the absolute silence found there. So, everyone begins to climb. Some with enthusiasm, others with fear, but they climb. The stairs are heavy, sometimes steep, but no one stops, because stopping is seen as failure.

And you climb, too. For years. But as you get closer, you realize you can't breathe well. You don't see what the others see. The tower doesn't call to you; it weighs on you. And one day, you stop. You sit on a step and look down, not up. You realize you don't want to reach the top. That the tower isn't yours. That the view holds no attraction for you. And that meaning is not found at the heights, but in the depth of your choice.

Society tells you that you must keep climbing: have a specific career, get married, have children. But you understand that not all paths lead upward. Some lead inward. And staying on your own step—with lucidity, with peace, with your choice—is sometimes more courageous than climbing without knowing why.

Chapter 15

The Emotional Baggage

„I am not what happened to me. I am what I choose to become."

Carl Jung

Every relationship begins with two people. But in reality, there are many more invisible presences at the table: each person's inner child, their parents, past relationships, traumas, fears, unfulfilled desires, and silent shames. All of these form the emotional baggage: that set of experiences, beliefs, and wounds that remain unseen but are felt in every interaction.

Emotional baggage is not a burden we must hide, but a part of our emotional identity. It is what causes us to react disproportionately, to withdraw, to defend ourselves, or to cling. It is what makes us love with fear or with intensity, to ask without knowing what we need, and perhaps to run away precisely when we feel longing.

In a couple, this baggage becomes activated. Not because the partner provokes it, but because emotional closeness brings to the surface everything that has been buried. The relationship becomes a mirror—sometimes gentle, sometimes painful—in which we see ourselves as we truly are, not as we imagine ourselves to be.

Every human being enters a relationship with a story. Not just with what they say, but especially with what they *don't* say. With what they do not yet know about themselves. With that which was wounded, lost, neglected, abandoned, or idealized. With what they have learned to hide, deny, or compensate for. This emotional baggage is expressed in gestures, in reactions, in absences, in the need for control, or in the flight from intimacy.

Often, what appears to be a couple's conflict is, in fact, a collision between two unhealed personal histories.

Emotional baggage is not a problem to be solved, but a reality to be understood. It is what makes us react excessively to a word spoken in haste. It is what makes us repeat patterns, choose partners who confirm our painful beliefs about ourselves, or flee from relationships that might actually heal us.

Becoming conscious of your own emotional baggage is an act of courage. It means stopping yourself from projecting it onto the other person. To stop asking your partner to fix what they did not break. To stop turning the relationship into a battlefield for old wounds. It means no longer confusing love with validation, rescue, or compensation. It means beginning to truly see yourself—to acknowledge what you carry, to understand why you react the way you do, and to accept that sometimes, it is the pain speaking instead of you.

In a couple, emotional baggage can be a source of conflict, but it is also an opportunity for growth. If ignored, it becomes a weight that presses down on the relationship—a latent tension manifesting as repetitive arguments, distancing, and misunderstandings that seem minor but have deep roots. However, if viewed with sincerity, it becomes a bridge between partners. It becomes an invitation to vulnerability, to listening, and to learning a common emotional language. It allows for a relationship where each person takes responsibility for what they bring to the table without blaming the other.

Emotional baggage does not disappear. But it can be carried differently: with more awareness, more kindness, less shame, and more responsibility. Relationships are not built on ideals, but on shared truths. And the truth about who we really are begins when we look inside and acknowledge what we have been carrying for years without even knowing it.

Depending on the content of this emotional baggage—especially its painful components—there can be a profound impact on the family's balance. Unhealed wounds, unspoken fears, and unprocessed losses do not remain in the past; they seep into the present of the relationship. They become filters through which each partner perceives reality, reacts to challenges, and interprets gestures. Without awareness, these filters can deeply distort the couple's dynamics.

Perhaps the most delicate and decisive effect of emotional baggage manifests in one's parenting style. Once a child enters a couple's life, not only is love amplified, but so are vulnerabilities. A child does not arrive in a neutral space, but in a pre-existing emotional context shaped by each parent's history. That context—whether harmonious or strained, conscious or reactive—becomes the environment in which the child will grow and learn the meaning of safety, love, boundaries, and trust.

A parent carrying misunderstood pain may become hyper-protective or, conversely, distant. They might project their own unfulfilled dreams, fears, or expectations onto the child. They may demand that the child be "good," "obedient," or "perfect"—not for the child's sake, but to soothe their own inner restlessness. They might react disproportionately to a child's mistakes, not because the errors are grave, but because they touch an old, unclosed wound. Thus, a parenting style is not just a conscious choice; it is an expression of the parent's inner world.

Furthermore, the child *feels* it. Even if they cannot understand it rationally, they perceive the tensions, the emotional absences, and the misalignment between what is said and what is lived. Children are extremely sensitive to the affective atmosphere of the family. They absorb not just words, but moods, gestures, and silences. They grow in that emotional soil, and if the soil is unstable, the child will learn to adapt, to protect themselves, and to conform—often at the cost of their own authenticity.

Therefore, emotional baggage is not just a personal matter; it is a transgenerational one. How it is managed (or ignored) will influence not only the couple's relationship but the child's entire future. It will shape how they relate to themselves, to others, and to the world. It will become part of their story, even if they don't know exactly where it came from.

Looking honestly at one's emotional baggage is not a selfish act; it is a profoundly generous one. It is a form of affective responsibility. It is a choice not to pass on what has not been healed. Authentic presence begins where the adult acknowledges their wounds and chooses not to let them take the lead.

15.1. Fears

Fears are not always shouted. Most of the time, they slip into a relationship in silence, camouflaged as seemingly logical reasons, in postponed decisions, or in disproportionate reactions. In a couple, each partner arrives with their own terrors—some conscious, others deeply buried. The fear of not being enough, the fear of repeating the mistakes of one's parents, the fear of losing freedom, the fear of not knowing how to love a child, the fear of being rejected, of being overwhelmed, or of being transformed into a version that no longer resembles the authentic self.

These fears are not signs of weakness; they are signs of humanity. They appear not only in moments of crisis but also in moments of decision—especially when the perspective of parenthood opens up. When the idea of bringing a child into the world becomes real rather than theoretical, these fears activate. This happens not because the partner provokes them, but because the future becomes a mirror in which each person sees their own limits, their own wounds, and their own unanswered questions.

The partners' fears may differ, but they influence one another. One may feel the need for control, while the other feels the need for space. One may desire a child as a form of fulfillment, while the other may see it as a threat to an already fragile balance. One may feel they will become more alive, more connected, more whole; the other may feel they will be suffocated, lost, or redefined in a way that doesn't belong to them. If these fears are not put into words, they transform into tensions, indirect reproaches, half-hearted decisions, and conflicts that have nothing to do with the present, but with the past.

Fears do not disappear if they are ignored; they intensify. They manifest through withdrawal, defensiveness, sarcasm, or silence. They infiltrate small gestures, the refusal to speak about the future, the avoidance of the topic of children, and the need to maintain control over time, space, and the body. Without awareness, these fears can sabotage a relationship, even when love is present.

Fears can also be bridges. If they are recognized, shared, and listened to without judgment, they can become the beginning of true intimacy. Saying "I am afraid" does not mean being weak; it means being sincere. Saying "I don't know if I will be a good parent" is not an act of running away; it is the courage to look a massive responsibility in the face. Saying "I am afraid of losing myself" can open a vital conversation about identity, personal space, and balance.

In a couple, fears should not be banished but understood. They don't need to be solved immediately, but *contained.* Sometimes, the simple act of speaking them aloud makes them easier to carry. In the context of parenthood, talking about fears is an act of responsibility. A child does not need parents who feel no fear, but parents who know what to do with it.

Fears are not obstacles; they are signs. They show us where it hurts, where healing is needed, and where support is required. If viewed with kindness, patience, and maturity, they can lead to a deeper relationship: with oneself, with one's partner, and with the future.

Not everyone recognizes their fears. Some deny them firmly: "I have no fears. I am just a realist." But fear does not only express itself through trembling or panic. It slips into behaviors, choices, and avoidances.

The fears of partners do not announce themselves loudly. They don't carry signs or demand attention. They creep into the relationship in silence, hidden in gestures, hesitations, and remarks that seem rational but carry an unspoken unease. Each partner brings their own baggage—sometimes conscious, sometimes locked away in a corner of memory. The fear of not being enough, of not knowing how to love, of not being able to protect or provide stability. The fear of being transformed by responsibility, of being overwhelmed, or of losing freedom.

There are people who say with conviction: "I have no fear." But fear hides in the need for control, in the refusal to speak about the future, and in the sarcasm that appears when a conversation becomes too serious. It hides in excessive work, in the avoidance of vulnerability, and in the desire to keep everything "under control." It manifests through the need to plan every detail, through the refusal to take concrete steps, and through the dread of being asked: "What do you feel?"

There is the fear of failing as a parent—a deep terror that is not easily voiced. The fear that you won't know how to protect, educate, or love without causing harm. The fear that you will repeat your parents' mistakes, passing on exactly what you have tried so hard to heal. The fear that you will be too harsh, too absent, or too confused. Or, conversely, too permissive, too dependent, or too vulnerable. This fear paralyzes because it offers no clear answers. No one can guarantee they will be a "good" parent. It is precisely this uncertainty that causes some to withdraw, to postpone, and to avoid.

Then, there is the fear of being abandoned within the relationship—of becoming invisible in the eyes of the partner, especially after the child arrives. The fear of no longer being chosen, no longer being desired, or being replaced by a new form of love that does not include you. This fear manifests as subtle jealousy, a constant need for reassurance, and tensions that may not seem related to the child but have everything to do with them. For some, the idea of a child awakens not just responsibility, but a profound dread that the relationship will transform into a mere logistical partnership, that love will be redistributed, and that intimacy will be lost.

And there is a fear even harder to admit: the fear of the child itself. Of the unknown they bring. Of the mirror they will hold up to your face. Of the questions they will raise and the challenges that cannot be anticipated. Some fear they won't know how to connect, that they won't feel love as expected, that they will be rejected, or overwhelmed by a relationship they cannot control. This fear is not about the child; it is about what the child brings to the surface within *you*.

All these fears are natural. They are not signs of weakness, but of awareness. They should not be banished, but understood; not solved immediately, but *contained.* Sometimes, the simple act of naming them makes them easier to carry. In a couple, speaking about these fears is an act of maturity—not to eliminate them, but to integrate them. A child does not need perfect parents; they need parents who know what to do with their own shadows.

Fears do not always look like fears. Sometimes they camouflage as solid reasoning, as postponed decisions, or as pragmatic remarks. Other times they hide in silences, in jokes, or in restlessness. In a couple, each partner arrives with their own anxieties. Even if one says with conviction, "I have no fear," the inner reality is more complex. Fear isn't just trembling or withdrawal; it is the need to control everything, the refusal to speak of the future, and the inability to sit in silence with an open question.

There is the fear of not being enough. At your job, where you feel you aren't performing well enough. Among friends, where you wonder if you are truly seen. In your relationship, where you fear you aren't interesting enough, mature enough, or worthy enough of love. In the relationship with your parents, where you still carry the desire to be validated, appreciated, and considered a "success." This fear manifests through constant effort, perfectionism, comparisons, and exhaustion. Paradoxically, the harder you strive to be enough, the further you feel from yourself.

Then, there is the fear of losing control—in your relationship, your career, your body, and your life. The need to know what's next, to anticipate, to plan, and to prevent. But control is often an illusion; life does not allow itself to be framed into spreadsheets. When the idea of a child arises, this fear intensifies. Nothing is more unpredictable than a new soul. If you haven't learned to adapt, to be flexible, and to let yourself be surprised, the fear of losing control becomes suffocating. It manifests as rigidity, a refusal to take steps forward, and the constant need for a Plan B, C, or D.

Fears do not come alone; they are interlinked and feed off one another. The fear of repeating your parents' mistakes is one of the most painful. It isn't just about the future; it's about the past. It's about what you lived through, what you learned, and what you swore you would never do. Yet, in moments of vulnerability, exhaustion, or crisis, those exact patterns emerge. And then you wonder if you are truly different. If you can break the chain. If you can build something else.

Finally, there is the fear of real intimacy—of being truly seen. Of being known beyond the surface. Of being asked, "What do you feel?" and not knowing how to answer. Many settle for surface-level conversations, jokes, logistical plans, and discussions about what to eat for dinner. It's safe there. You don't risk being hurt. But real intimacy requires courage, presence, and availability. The fear of being vulnerable, being rejected, or being considered "too complicated" causes some partners to remain in the comfortable zone of the superficial.

Fears intensify in the face of the unknown. And nothing is more unknown than the future—the idea of a child, of transformation, of responsibility, and redefinition. Some fear they won't know how to love. Others fear they will be overwhelmed. Some fear they will feel nothing; others, that they will feel too much. The unknown cannot be controlled; it can only be traversed. It is precisely this lack of guarantees that causes some to freeze, to postpone, and to avoid.

Perhaps the most subtle fear is that of missing out on one's own life. The fear of making wrong choices, of walking a path that leads nowhere, or of living a life that isn't truly yours. The fear of waking up years from now with the feeling that you were absent from your own story. This fear is not easily voiced; it is felt in a constant restlessness, a need for change, and a hunger for meaning. Sometimes, the idea of a child seems to deepen this fear because it brings with it an irreversible choice—a clear direction and a responsibility that can no longer be renegotiated.

All these fears are natural. They should not be denied or hidden. They are not obstacles, but signs. Signs that you are alive, that you care, and that you want to choose consciously. If they are spoken, shared, and contained, they can become the beginning of a deeper relationship—with yourself, with your partner, and with life itself.

There is also the fear of being betrayed—not just as physical infidelity, but as the loss of emotional exclusivity. It is the feeling that you are no longer the one being chosen, seen, or desired. This fear can be activated subtly, without evidence or clear suspicion. It is felt in moments when the partner seems distant, in those seconds when that specific gaze—the one that once said "you are mine"—is missing. It manifests through silent jealousy, a constant need for reassurance, and unasked questions that weigh heavy. When the idea of a child enters the landscape, this fear can become even more intense. It brings with it a new kind of vulnerability, a deeper emotional dependency, and a need for stability that makes any perceived threat feel significantly more dangerous.

Equally powerful is the fear of raising a child alone—of being abandoned at the exact moment you need support the most. The fear of being left with the entire responsibility: the sleepless nights, the hard decisions, the unanswered questions. This fear is not just about the partner; it is about life itself. It is about how unpredictable life can be and how fragile safety truly is. Even if the relationship seems solid, this fear can arise as a memory of stories heard, a projection of dark scenarios, or a question that cannot be ignored: *"What do I do if I am left alone?"*

All these fears—of not being enough, of losing control, of repeating the parents' mistakes, of real intimacy, of the unknown, of missing out on life, of betrayal, or of being alone with a child—are not signs of weakness. They are signs that you are aware. That you care. That you want to choose with maturity. They should not be denied but understood; not solved immediately, but *contained*. Because a child does not need perfect parents, but parents who know what to do with their own shadows. And a couple does not need certainties, but the courage to traverse the unknown together.

These fears are human. We should not be ashamed of them, nor should we hide them. They do not define us, but they accompany us. They are signs that we want to choose well, that we desire a life of meaning. Because they are natural, they deserve to be viewed with kindness, not judgment. To be spoken, not denied. To be contained, not banished. The moment we acknowledge them, they begin to transform. They do not disappear, but they no longer lead us. They no longer sabotage us. They no longer hold us back.

Life cannot be lived based on the principle of "what if the sky falls." We cannot postpone joy, love, decisions, or hope just because there is a risk of pain. Fear protects us, but it can also paralyze us. If we remain stuck in scenarios, calculations, and avoidances, we risk waking up to find we have lived only half a life. The fear of death, so present in many souls, is often merely the reflex of an unlived life—of an existence where we were more spectators than participants.

Liberation does not come from the absence of fear, but from the courage to live with it. To take it by the hand and step forward anyway. With joy. With presence. With the confidence that life is worth living, even when we do not have all the answers.

15.2. Losses

Every person enters a relationship with a history. And within that history, there are losses: some visible, others silent. The loss of loved ones, the loss of relationships that left scars the loss of trust, stability, or meaning. Sometimes, loss is not about death, but about absence. It's about someone who wasn't there when you needed them. About a love that faded without explanation. About a friendship that broke. About a dream that collapsed. About a part of you that was lost along the way.

These losses do not end with the arrival of a new partner. They are not erased; instead, they move into the background. They are reactivated in moments of vulnerability, in gestures that mirror the past, or in silences that remind us of other silences. If they are not recognized, they can become obstacles in the relationship. They can create mistrust, reactivity, and defensiveness. They can make one partner fear abandonment even when there is no real sign of it, or fear intimacy because closeness was once followed by pain.

Some have lost parents, either physically or emotionally. They grew up with absence, with a longing to be seen, and a need to be protected. Others have lost important relationships that shook their faith in love. Some have endured painful breakups, betrayals, or ruptures that made them wonder if it's still worth opening up. Others have lost children through miscarriages, failed pregnancies, or difficult decisions. Still others have lost versions of themselves: they gave up on dreams, freedom, or spontaneity to survive in an environment that didn't understand them.

All these losses are alive. They are not just memories, but emotional structures that influence the present. And in the context of parenthood, they become even more relevant. As a child does not just enter a physical space, but an affective one. And that space is shaped by what was lost, what was healed, and what was hidden. If the pain has not been processed, it can be transmitted. Not through words, but through gestures, reactions, and absences. The child may unknowingly become an attempt at compensation. Or, conversely, a source of fear: the fear of losing again, the fear of not being enough, the fear of repeating the past.

To speak of loss does not mean to remain stuck in the past. It means recognizing what you carry with you. Understanding how it has changed you. Seeing what you have learned, what you have lost, and what you have gained. It means creating a space within the relationship where pain is not shameful, but human. Where vulnerability is not a weakness, but a bridge. Where each partner can tell their story without fear of being judged or rejected.

Because, ultimately, our losses do not make us less capable of love. They make us more aware. More attentive. More profound. And if they are viewed with honesty, they can become sources of wisdom. They can transform a relationship into a space for healing. They can ensure that a future child grows up in an environment where pain is not denied, but understood—where love is not idealized, but lived in all its nuances.

When we speak of loss, the mind often drifts toward death—the definitive absence of a loved one. But loss has many faces. Some are silent, others invisible, yet all leave a mark. Before two people meet, form a couple, and become parents, each comes with their own inventory of losses. And that inventory does not evaporate with the arrival of love. On the contrary, it reactivates, rewrites itself, and demands to be understood.

A loss may be:

- The Loss of Property or Belongings – Which carries with it a sense of instability, insecurity, and a rupture in the continuity of one's life.

- The Loss of a Job – Which represents not just the loss of income, but also the loss of status, identity, and a sense of purpose.
- The Loss of a Friendship – Whether through emotional distancing or an unresolved conflict, leaving behind unanswered questions, longing, and sometimes, guilt.
- The Loss of Prestige or Reputation – A subtle form of social exclusion that can deeply affect self-confidence and the capacity to feel seen and valued.
- The Loss of a Version of Oneself – Giving up on a dream, a freedom, or a part of one's identity in order to adapt, to survive, or to be accepted.

All these losses are real. They are measured not by their intensity, but by their impact. And their impact is felt within the relationship. It is felt in how someone reacts to uncertainty, to rejection, or to change. It is felt in the need for control, the fear of abandonment, and the difficulty of opening up. It manifests in the way a partner relates to money, work, friends, and themselves.

In the context of parenthood, these losses become even more relevant. A child does not arrive in an empty space, but in a space already heavy with emotional history. If losses remain unprocessed, they can become ghosts that haunt the relationship. They can create tensions, projections, and disproportionate reactions. They can cause a parent to fear losing the child, fear not being enough, or fear repeating the mistakes of the past.

However, if recognized, these losses can become sources of wisdom. They can bring depth, empathy, and the capacity to understand the pain of another. They can transform the relationship into a space of healing. They can ensure that a future child grows up in an environment where pain is not denied, but understood—where loss is not a taboo subject, but a part of life.

Regardless of the nature of the loss—be it human, material, relational, symbolic, or a loss of status, physical, or emotional freedom—the soul needs time and space to process it. Loss is not just a rupture; it is a transition. And this transition requires a process of grieving. We grieve not only in the face of death but also when we lose a relationship, a dream, an identity, a freedom, or a choice.

Elisabeth Kübler-Ross described five stages of grief that apply not only to death but to any significant loss. These stages are not rigid or linear; they can overlap, repeat, and alternate. Everyone experiences them differently, depending on the depth of the loss and their capacity to confront pain.

Denial is the first natural reaction—the moment when the mind refuses to accept reality. One might say: *"This can't be happening to me," "Everything will go back to normal,"* or *"It's not really that serious."* It is a form of psychological protection, a defense mechanism that cushions the shock. In a relationship, denial may appear as an avoidance of difficult conversations or an escape into work, activities, and distractions.

Anger arrives when reality begins to assert itself. It is a visceral reaction, sometimes directed at others, at oneself, or at life. One might ask: *"Why me?", "Who is to blame?",* or *"How did I allow this?"* In a couple, anger can be projected onto the partner, even if they have no direct connection to the loss. It may manifest as irritability, mistrust, or constant tension.

Bargaining is the stage where one attempts to regain control. It is a subtle form of hope and illusion. One might think: *"If I do* *everything better, more responsibly, maybe things will be fixed,"* or *"If I admit I was wrong somewhere, maybe I can learn from this."* In a relationship, bargaining can manifest as over-adaptation—making disproportionate efforts to please, avoid conflict, or maintain appearances.

Depression is the moment when the pain truly settles in. It is the stage where one feels the void, the lack, and the absence. One may become withdrawn, apathetic, or overwhelmed, feeling that nothing makes sense anymore, that the future is uncertain, and that there is no energy left to continue. In a couple, this stage can bring emotional distancing, communication difficulties, and a need for isolation.

Acceptance does not mean forgetting; it means integration. It is the stage where one acknowledges the loss as part of their own story. One begins to build anew, rediscovering meaning and reconnecting with life. In a relationship, acceptance brings maturity, depth, and the capacity to be present without fleeing from the past. It is the moment when the pain is no longer an open wound, but a scar that speaks of survival.

To allow grief to manifest means giving pain permission to be seen. It means not hiding it under performance, smiles, or the mantra of "I must be strong." It means creating a space where each partner can say: "I have lost something. And it still hurts." This is an act of courage, but also an act of love. Because it is only through grieving that loss is transformed: from a wound into wisdom, from a void into space for something new, and from fear into compassion.

In some communities, especially rural or traditional ones, outward mourning—such as wearing black clothes—extends far beyond the ritual period. There are people who choose to wear black for years, believing this is how they honor the deceased.

Black becomes more than a color; it becomes a public declaration of pain, a form of loyalty to the past. However, beyond sincere respect, this choice can become a subtle brake on one's own life.

For some, prolonged mourning turns into a reason—conscious or not—for being absent from the present, for giving up on goals, relationships, or joy. It is as if they are saying: "I can't, I am still in mourning." But the truth is that you can honor a loved one while continuing your life. You can keep a memory alive without stopping yourself from living. Mourning should not be a sentence, but a stage. Life, with all its colors, deserves to be lived even after loss.

In situations where loss occurs suddenly, without the possibility of a conscious closure—without that "goodbye" that could have brought a shred of peace—open wounds, unanswered questions, and suspended emotions often remain.

For such moments, I propose a simple yet profound exercise that I learned during my training. It is a framework that allows for the sincere expression of pain, anger, need, and forgiveness, all related to a concrete situation that escalated and left its mark.

The **exercise** consists of completing four sentences, referring to the same person and the same context:

- You hurt me when...
- I was angry when...
- I would have wanted to tell you that...
- I forgive you / I do not forgive you because...

Written with sincerity, these sentences can become a ritual of symbolic closure. It is not necessary for the other person to hear them; it is enough for you to utter them, to write them, to feel them. Because, sometimes, healing begins where words never had the chance to be spoken.

The unspoken (that which remains unexpressed, unfinished, unsaid) transforms into an invisible burden that we carry day by day, without realizing how much it weighs us down. It is a subtle but constant tension that restrains our capacity to be present, to enjoy, to act. And perhaps the most disturbing effect of this burden is that, at the end of the day, our mind does not account for what we managed to do, but for what remained unfinished. What stays in our mind is the conversation that did not take place, the word that was not said, the gesture that was not made. And this accumulation of "unfinished things" becomes a background noise that weakens our confidence, disturbs our sleep, and keeps us blocked in a past that can no longer be changed, but which still controls our present.

15.3. Emotional wounds

The concept of "emotional wounds" was popularized by the Canadian psychologist Lise Bourbeau, who identified five fundamental types of wounds formed in childhood: rejection, abandonment, humiliation, betrayal, and injustice. These wounds are not simple passing emotions, but deep imprints that shape the way we relate to ourselves, to others, and to life in general.

Emotional wounds are formed in the parent-child relationship during moments of vulnerability, when the child does not have the capacity to correctly understand or process what is happening to them. A word spoken harshly, a repeated absence, or an invalidation of emotions—all can be experienced by the child as rejection or abandonment, even if the parent's intention was not such. For the child, the wound is not about what happened "in reality," but about how the experience was perceived and felt.

If these wounds are not made conscious and healed, they are reactivated in romantic relationships. The partner becomes, without knowing it, a "trigger" for old pain. Someone with an abandonment wound may become hypersensitive to distancing or lack of attention, interpreting neutral gestures as signs of withdrawal. Someone with a rejection wound may avoid intimacy for fear of being rejected again. Thus, the relationship is no longer a space for growth, but a battlefield with the ghosts of the past.

Moreover, these unhealed wounds can be transmitted transgenerationally. The wounded child, who becomes an adult and then a parent without having worked through their own pain, risks repeating the same patterns involuntarily. They may become hyper-protective, distant, critical, or emotionally unstable, not from a lack of love, but from an inability to offer what they did not receive. In this way, the wound perpetuates itself, and today's child becomes tomorrow's wounded adult.

Awareness is the first step toward healing. We cannot change what was, but we can learn to look toward the past with compassion, to understand our reactions, and to choose, consciously, not to let them lead our lives anymore—to rewrite the story.

• The rejection wound

The rejection wound often appears in the first years of life, when the child perceives that they are not wanted, accepted, or valued for who they are. It may involve an emotionally distant parent, one who is critical, or one overwhelmed by their own problems, failing to create a space of emotional safety. The child does not understand the context; they only feel that they are "not enough" or that they "have no place."

The adult with a rejection wound may become hypersensitive to any sign of disapproval, withdrawal, or lack of attention. They tend to isolate themselves, avoid conflicts, and withdraw before the other person can do so. They have difficulty asking, asserting themselves, or feeling truly seen. The relationship becomes a fragile ground where any gesture can be interpreted as rejection.

When becoming a parent, the adult with this wound may project their own fears onto the child. They may be excessively protective or, conversely, distant, for fear of causing harm. they may avoid expressing emotions or needs, creating a cold climate in which the child does not learn to feel unconditionally accepted. Thus, the wound can be transmitted subtly, but profoundly.

• The abandonment wound

This wound appears when the child feels that the attachment figure is not stable or present. It can involve physical absences (departures, divorces, hospitalizations), but also emotional absences: unavailable, preoccupied, or depressed parents. The child experiences a profound fear of being left alone, of not mattering.

The adult with an abandonment wound may become emotionally dependent and anxious, living with the fear that they will be deserted. They have a constant need for reassurance, presence, and proof of love. They may become suffocating or, paradoxically, may withdraw before the other person does, as a protection mechanism. The relationship becomes a dance between the need for closeness and the fear of loss.

As a parent, they may become over-involved, not allowing the child space for autonomy, or they may avoid deep attachment for fear of suffering again. They may project their own fears onto the child, demanding that the child always be present, loyal, or "good." Consequently, the child does not learn to feel free and safe within the relationship.

• The humiliation wound

This wound appears when the child is made to feel ashamed of who they are or what they feel. They may be ridiculed, criticized in public, compared to others, or punished for natural needs (such as the need for affection, exploration, or expression). They learn that vulnerability is dangerous and that they must hide.

The adult with a humiliation wound may have difficulty expressing themselves authentically. They fear judgment, shame, and being "too much" or "too little." They may become hyper-critical of themselves or their partner as a defense mechanism. The relationship can become a space of control, where vulnerability is avoided at all costs.

As a parent, they may transmit shame through critical remarks, irony, or comparisons. They may demand perfection, excessive discipline, or the inhibition of emotions. The child learns that they must be "correct," "well-behaved," or "acceptable," losing contact with their authenticity. The wound perpetuates itself through subtly transmitted shame.

• The betrayal wound

This wound appears when the child feels that their trust has been violated. It can involve broken promises, unstable parents, manipulation, or a lack of consistency between what is said and what is done. The child learns that they cannot rely on others and that they must maintain control to avoid being hurt.

The adult with a betrayal wound may become suspicious, controlling, jealous, or dominating. They have difficulty delegating, trusting, or relaxing within the relationship. They may constantly test their partner, seeking evidence of loyalty. The relationship becomes a field of verification, rather than trust.

As a parent, they may impose rigid rules, demand absolute loyalty, or be emotionally unstable without realizing it. The child learns that love is conditioned by behavior, and that they must "earn" trust. Thus, a strained relationship is formed, based on control rather than mutual trust.

- **The injustice wound**

This wound appears when the child feels they are not treated fairly, that they do not have the right to be who they are. They may be raised in a rigid, authoritarian environment where self-expression is sanctioned. They learn that they must conform, obey, and not cause trouble.

The adult with an injustice wound may become a perfectionist, rigid, and demanding of themselves and others. They have difficulty accepting mistakes and tolerating ambiguity or vulnerability. They may feel they do not receive "what they deserve" and frequently feel wronged. The relationship becomes a space of evaluation rather than acceptance.

As a parent, they may impose high standards and be critical or inflexible. They may demand the child be "correct," "moral," or "exemplary," without allowing them to make mistakes or explore. The child learns that love comes with conditions and that they must conform to be accepted. Thus, the wound is transmitted through rigidity and a lack of empathy.

Introspection Exercise: A Letter to the Parent Who Caused the Wound

For those who feel they carry within them an emotional wound formed in the relationship with one of their parents, I propose a conscious writing exercise: a letter that does not have to be sent, but which can be written with sincerity, courage, and the desire to release what was left unsaid. It is a process of emotional "emptying" that brings clarity and can open the way toward healing.

Instructions:

Choose a quiet moment when you feel safe. Take a notebook or a sheet of paper and write a letter addressed to the parent (or parents) who caused the wound. Do not censor yourself. Do not try to be "correct" or "balanced." Write from within, with the voice of the child who was not heard, with the voice of the adolescent who felt alone, with the voice of the adult who is trying to understand.

Here are some helpful questions regarding what you can include in the letter:

- The first memory related to that wound: What happened? How did you feel in that moment? What would you have needed to happen instead?
- Other similar situations: When did the wound repeat itself? How did you react? How did your parents react? What did you learn about yourself?
- The transformation in adolescence and adulthood: How did the wound affect you in your relationships? In your

self-confidence? In the way you related to love, authority, and vulnerability?

- Reflection on your romantic relationship: What patterns have you observed? What did you demand or avoid? What did you project onto your partner?
- What you would like to say now: What have you never said? What would you have wanted them to hear? What do you need to release?

The letter does not have to be perfect. It can be fragmented, emotional, or contradictory. It can be written in several stages. It can be burned, kept, or reread. The important thing is that it is written. Because, sometimes, the words we did not say keep us stuck in the past. And uttering them, even on paper, can be the first step toward freedom.

If the possibility exists, the person writing the letter may choose to deliver it orally to the parent who caused the wound. It is not an easy gesture, but it can be profoundly healing—not to obtain apologies, but to affirm one's own story, to make oneself heard.

If this is not possible or if the person in question does not feel safe doing so, the letter can be read aloud only by the author. Hearing yourself utter what you have written brings an extra layer of awareness and validation of the pain experienced. It is as if you are saying: "This is my story. I am no longer running from it. I am looking it in the face."

Writing is more than a creative act; it is a space for inner clarification, a safe ground where thoughts can be settled, emotions can be understood, and wounds can be explored without haste.

Keeping a journal does not mean writing daily or following a specific form. It means creating a sincere dialogue with yourself, noting what you feel, what you dream of, what hurts you, and what brings you joy. In time, the journal becomes a map of your transformation, a silent witness to the journey taken.

Among the benefits of conscious writing are: the reduction of anxiety by expressing thoughts that would otherwise remain jumbled, the clarification of decisions and relationships, reconnecting with the authentic self, and creating a space for reflection and gratitude.

Chapter 16

Healthy Motivation: The child as an expression of love and maturity

---

„When parents understand their own story, they can write a new one for their children."
Dr. Daniel Siegel

There is a special kind of silence that precedes the decision to have a child. It is not an oppressive silence, but a full one, like a deep breath before a leap. It is the silence in which two people look at each other and know, without speaking, that their love has reached a point where it can create without asking, give without conditioning, and accompany without controlling. It is the moment when the child is no longer a solution, nor a salvation, nor a promise, but an expression. A living form of a love.

This motivation is not born out of lack, but out of abundance. It does not come from a need for validation, but from a desire to share. It is not impulsive, nor rushed, but mature, settled, and conscious. It is a choice that is not made lightly, but is made with clarity. Having a child out of mature love means receiving them as a distinct being, not as an extension of the self. It means looking at them with clear eyes, not through the lenses of one's own unfulfilled dreams. It means accompanying them in their becoming, not molding them according to the contours of our desires.

Maturity is not a state of perfection, but a capacity to be present. To recognize one's own wounds without projecting them. To accept that we will not be flawless parents, but we will be able to be authentic parents. It is the courage to look at ourselves in the child's mirror without running, without hiding, without demanding that they be different so that we can feel okay. It is the willingness to learn, to make mistakes, to ask for forgiveness, and to grow together with them.

A child born from this motivation will feel that they are wanted, not necessary. That they are loved, not used. That they are free, not conditioned. They will grow in an emotional space where mistakes are not punishments, but opportunities for learning; where emotions are not denied, but contained; where freedom is not a danger, but a promise. They will learn that love is not earned, but given. That they do not have to be someone else to be accepted, but that they are enough just as they are.

This motivation is the only one that does not transform the child into a means to an end. It does not force them to become someone just so the parent can feel fulfilled. It does not burden them with invisible weights, unspoken expectations, or unshared desires. It is the only one that does not demand, but offers. It does not project, but accepts. It does not condition, but supports. It is a motivation that does not come from fear, but from love; not from a need for control, but from a willingness to accompany; not from a desire to fill a void, but from the joy of sharing a sense of wholeness.

Perhaps, in the end, the true inheritance we can leave is not a perfect education, nor a list of achievements, nor a meticulously planned future—but a model of love that does not crush, but uplifts. A model of maturity that does not impose, but inspires. A space where the child can become who they are, not who they should have been. A space where life is not a competition, but a journey; where the parent is not an architect, but a witness; where love is not a strategy, but a presence.

Having a child out of mature love is, perhaps, the most profound form of creation. Not because it gives birth to a life, but because it gives birth to a relationship in which both—parent and child—can become more than they were before. It is a choice that is not made lightly, but is made with truth. And in that truth, the child is not a burden, nor a mission, nor a projection. They are a being who comes simply to *be* and who, in the mature love of their parents, will learn that being is enough.

The child desired out of pure love—without pressure, without masked ambitions, without the desire to repair the past or save the present—is raised under a silent but profound mission: "I wish to raise a child who will become a free and independent adult." Not free in the superficial sense of material autonomy, but free in thought, in feeling, and in choice. An adult who will not be a prisoner of parental expectations, nor of inherited fears, nor of the need to prove something to someone. An adult who will be able to say "no" without guilt and "yes" without fear.

This mission is not about forming a "good," "well-behaved," or "high-achieving" child, but about accompanying them in their authentic becoming. It is about creating a space where the child can explore, make mistakes, question, challenge, and dream. A space where the parent is not an architect drawing rigid lines, but a gardener providing fertile soil, light, and patience. It is about cultivating in the child the ability to listen to themselves, to recognize their needs, and to build their own moral and emotional landmarks.

Raising a child with their future independence in mind means, paradoxically, being willing to withdraw. To accept that, one day, they will leave. That they will choose differently than you would have chosen. That they will love differently, think differently, and live differently. And that all of these are not failures, but signs that you have succeeded—that you have raised a person who is not afraid to be themselves.

This motivation requires a rare form of generosity: that of not demanding gratitude. Of not waiting for the love offered to return in the form of confirmation. Of not transforming the child into a guarantor of one's own worth. It is a love that does not keep score, does not negotiate, and does not manipulate. It is a love that says: "I love you because you exist, not because you do something in particular."

In such a relationship, the child learns that freedom is not a threat, but a responsibility. That love is not a reward, but a constant. That a mistake is not the end of the road, but a part of the road. And, above all, they learn that they can be who they are without losing the love of those who raised them.

To love maturely means being willing to give up the image of the ideal child, your projections, and the desire to see them "successful" by your standards. It means looking at them with clear eyes, listening without immediate correction, and letting them formulate their own questions, even if their answers do not resemble yours. It is a love that does not rush to intervene, but learns to wait. One that does not say "I know better," but asks "how do you see things?"

In daily life, this love translates into seemingly small, yet perhaps decisive gestures: in respecting the child's rhythm, in not comparing them to others, and in not pressuring them to perform in order to be accepted. It is seen in how the parent reacts to the child's failure—not with disappointment, but with encouragement; not with reproach, but with understanding. It is seen in the ability to say "I don't know," "I was wrong," or "I'm sorry," because maturity does not fear vulnerability, but integrates it.

Mature love is not a love that imposes itself, but one that offers itself. It is not a love that controls, but one that accompanies. It manifests not only in moments of joy, but especially in times of crisis—when the child rebels, shuts down, or pulls away. In those moments, the mature parent does not react with panic or authority, but with patience and a deep trust in the growth process. They know that autonomy does not come from obedience, but from exploration.

This love does not fear division. It does not cling to the child, nor does it keep them confined in the role of "my little one." It slowly prepares them for departure. It teaches them how to manage, how to decide, how to doubt, and how to reconfigure themselves. It offers them both roots and wings. It says to them, without words: "You are not mine. You are yours. I am here as long as you need me, but I will not be the wall that stops you. I will be the bridge that lets you cross."

In such a relationship, the child learns that love is not a burden, but a support; that the parent is not a judge, but a witness; that a mistake is not a shame, but a part of the path. And, above all, they learn that they can be who they are without losing the love of those who raised them.

Parents who choose to bring a child into the world out of pure love, maturity, and awareness are not parents without fears. On the contrary, they are parents who recognize their vulnerability, who feel anxiety, and who wonder if they are doing enough, if they are making mistakes, or if their child is okay. But what sets them apart is how they express these concerns. They do not raise their voices, they do not accuse, and they do not project fear in the form of reproach. They do not say "you disappointed me," but instead ask "what happened?", "how did you feel?", or "what did you need that you didn't receive?".

These parents understand that worry should not become a weapon, but an opportunity for closeness; that their emotion should not crush, but open up; that their reaction should not frighten, but invite dialogue. They choose to communicate assertively—honestly and gently. Clearly, yet adapted to the child's level of understanding. They do not speak "down" to them, but "beside" them. They do not impose; they explain. They do not demand submission; they cultivate trust.

In such a climate, the child learns that a mistake is not a betrayal, but an opportunity to learn; that the parent is not a judge waiting for perfection, but a partner who understands the process. They learn that love does not withdraw in difficult moments, but draws closer. The parent's fear does not turn into anger, but into care expressed with respect.

These parents are not afraid to say "I am worried about what is happening," but they do so without burdening the child with guilt. They do not say "I don't sleep at night because of you," but rather

"I would like to understand what is going on with you, because I care." They do not say "you are making me suffer," but "I am affected by what you are going through and I want to be by your side." It is a communication that does not manipulate, but builds; it does not break, but binds.

In this type of relationship, the child learns that they can talk about what they feel without being punished; that they can admit a mistake without being humiliated; that they can ask for help without being considered weak. And, above all, they learn that love is not a bargaining chip, but a safe space where they can truly be themselves.

In relationships built on mature love, a mistake is not the end of the road, but a natural part of the learning process. The child is allowed to make mistakes, not as a concession, but as recognition that development is not linear, but full of hesitations, trials, and steps back. Making a mistake does not mean failing; it means exploring limits, testing hypotheses, and learning about consequences. It is an act of courage, not a shame.

The mature parent does not react to a mistake with panic or punishment, but with presence. They do not ask "how could you do this?", but "what did you learn from what happened?". They do not say "you disappointed me," but "let's see together what you felt and what you need now." In this climate, the child learns that a mistake is not a threat to love, but an opportunity to be understood.

This approach does not mean blind permissiveness, but cultivated responsibility. The child is not left to repeat mistakes without guidance, but is taught to look at them with lucidity, to analyze them, and to transform them into personal lessons. They are taught to take ownership, not to hide; to repair, not to avoid; to ask for help, not to isolate themselves.

In such an environment, the child is not afraid to try. They do not get stuck in perfectionism, nor do they hide for fear of being judged. They know that mistakes do not define them, but shape them. They know that the parent will not love them less for having made a mistake, but will accompany them more closely. They know they can be vulnerable without being weak. And, above all, they learn that life is not about avoiding mistakes, but about learning from them with dignity.

A mature parent does not see their child as an extension of their own life, but as a distinct being with their own paths and desires. They do not project unfulfilled dreams onto the child, nor do they transform the child's childhood into a revenge ground for their own failures. Instead, they offer space—that sacred space where the child can discover their dreams, shape them, change them, and follow them without the pressure of fulfilling someone else's expectations.

This does not mean the parent hides their past. On the contrary, they talk about their childhood, their dreams from back then, about what was and what wasn't. But they do so with an appropriate tone—without oppressive nostalgia, without subtle guilt, and without comparisons. Their story becomes a bridge, not a burden; an invitation to dialogue, not an imposed lesson.

The child listens and learns, but is not obligated to repair what the parent failed to achieve. They are not called to live a life that does not belong to them. They are encouraged to ask questions, to dream freely, and to choose. And the parent, instead of leading, accompanies. Instead of tracing directions, they offer landmarks. Instead of saying "I know what's best," they say "I am here if you need me."

In such a climate, the child's dream is not a replica of the parent's dream, but an authentic creation. It is an expression of the self, not a duty. It is a journey, not an imposed destination. And perhaps, precisely in this freedom, the parent finds their own dream again—not in its realization, but in the joy of having been a witness to the birth of another's dream.

A child does not come into the world to fit into a mold. They are not a piece in a pre-established puzzle, but a being in the making, with their own desires, curiosities, and rhythms. The mature parent understands that their role is not to draw outlines, but to offer support—to be there when the child explores, changes their mind, searches for themselves, and finds themselves.

In a healthy relationship, a child is not pushed to wear pink because they are a girl or blue because they are a boy. They are not encouraged to follow a profession just because "that's how it's done in our family." They are not conditioned to get married, to maintain the house, not to cry, to wear only skirts, or to be "strong" in the rigid sense of the word. All these stereotypes are replaced with authentic curiosity: "What do you like?", "How do you feel in these clothes?", "What truly attracts you?", "What does being yourself mean to you?".

The parent does not impose; they ask. They do not judge; they listen. They do not correct; they encourage. They are there as an anchor, not a conductor. And the child, feeling seen and accepted, has the courage to express themselves without fear. They can be a boy and cry. They can be a girl and not want to marry. They can be anything, as long as they are true to themselves.

This freedom does not mean chaos, but a profound respect for individuality. It means the parent does not fear difference, but celebrates it. They do not cling to blind tradition, but reinterpret it with discernment. They do not see their child as a continuation of their own identity, but as a new story that deserves to be written without censorship.

An emotionally mature parent is not the one who had a perfect childhood, but the one who chose not to repeat it. They are the one who looked their wounds in the face, named them, felt them, and understood them. They are the one who understood that the inherited emotional baggage does not have to be passed on, that pain does not have to become a tradition, and that suffering does not have to be perpetuated under the mask of "that's just how it's done."

This parent does not run from their past, but honors it through healing. They may have grown up in a cold, critical, abusive, or absent environment. They may have been taught that love is earned, that vulnerability is weakness, and that silence is safer than expression. But instead of repeating these patterns, they consciously choose to stop them. They choose to be present, gentle, and open. They choose not to react automatically, but to respond with discernment.

The process is not easy. Healing is not linear. Sometimes, old reflexes surface, pain is reactivated, and patience wears thin. But the difference is that the conscious parent observes, nuances, seeks support, and asks for forgiveness. They do not hide behind authority; they show their humanity. They are not afraid to say: "I am still learning. I am still healing. But I do not want to hurt you the way I was hurt."

This choice—not to repeat the model received—is an act of profound love. It is a quiet but powerful revolution. It is proof that pain can be transformed into care, that trauma can become wisdom, and that the past does not have to define the future. And a child raised in such an environment not only feels safe but learns, in turn, what mature love looks like: with clear boundaries, empathy, sincerity, and healing.

An emotionally mature parent does not view the child as an obstacle to their dreams, but as a natural and profound part of their own becoming. They do not say "you messed up my life," but "my life reconfigured itself along with you." They do not cling to what could have been, but embrace what is, with adaptability, lucidity, and love.

Being a parent does not mean giving up on yourself, but finding yourself in a new form. The mature parent does not abandon personal goals; they reinterpret them. They may no longer have the same time, the same freedom, or the same energy, but they have an additional motivation: the child becomes a source of meaning, an impulse to keep going, to build, and to leave behind a model worthy of following.

And this is precisely where the difference lies: the parent does not preach; they live. They do not give lectures on ambition, courage, or perseverance, but demonstrate them day by day through their own example. The child sees how the parent rises after failure, how they maintain their dignity in hard times, and how they continue to learn, create, and love. They learn not from words, but from presence, from deeds, and from actions.

This attitude does not come from idealism, but from a conscious choice. The mature parent knows that life is not a straight line, but a succession of reconfigurations. And in each reconfiguration, the child is not an obstacle, but a lighthouse; not a limitation, but a revelation; not a burden, but an opportunity to become more authentic, more profound, and more alive.

The mature parent does not position themselves as the absolute holder of truth, but as a partner on the journey who, despite having more landmarks, continues to learn. Faced with a difficult situation, they do not say "I know better," but "let's see together what we can understand from this." They do not impose; they propose. They do not dictate; they dialogue.

Of course, the parent can express their opinion, and it is important to do so. But they do it with modesty, openness, and a willingness to be contradicted. They do not demand the automatic application of their point of view, but invite the child to think, to feel, and to decide. In this way, the child learns not just to listen, but to reflect, to argue, and to take ownership of their choices.

This attitude cultivates self-confidence in the child and respect for others. It teaches them that opinions can coexist, that difference is not a threat, but an opportunity for learning. It teaches them that the parent is not a judge, but a human being who makes mistakes, corrects themselves, wonders, and transforms.

In such a climate, the child is not afraid to say "I don't agree." They do not feel guilty for thinking differently. They know that love does not depend on conformity, but on authenticity. They know they can contribute to solutions, not just execute them. And, perhaps most importantly, they learn that healthy relationships are built on mutual listening, not on submission.

The family climate created by conscious and emotionally mature parents is one that is affectionate, full of love, safety, and authentic presence. It is not a perfect space, but a living one, where mistakes are accepted, differences are celebrated, and relationships are built with patience and sincerity.

It is like caring for a flower. You don't just settle for watering it now and then; you ensure it has fertile soil, full of nutrients. You place it in the light, offer it warmth, and protect it from winds that are too strong. And, when you notice its roots have grown and need more space, you are not afraid to change its pot. You give it room to expand, to strengthen, and to bloom.

That is how a child is in such an environment: they are not forced to stay small, nor pushed to grow up too fast. They are accompanied. They are observed with care, not with control; supported, not molded. And the parent, like an attentive gardener, does not rush or impose, but cultivates with love, patience, and wisdom.

In such a climate, the child flourishes not because they were told how to be, but because they were allowed to be. And the parent, watching that flower grow, feels no possessive pride, but a profound joy: the joy of having been a witness and a support in the becoming of a free being.

16.1 Implications and Consequences

When a child is raised in an emotionally mature family climate, the consequences are felt far beyond the walls of the home. The parent who has consciously chosen not to repeat the painful patterns of their own childhood, who knows their wounds and works on healing them, becomes not just a support, but a living model of transformation. The relationship with the child is not one of control, but of accompaniment. It is based not on rigid authority, but on mutual respect, listening, and presence. In this process, the parent heals and redefines themselves, learning to be flexible, to adapt, and to reconfigure their life without seeing the child as an obstacle, but as an additional motivation to move forward with meaning.

For the child, this type of relationship is the foundation of healthy development. They learn that they are loved not for what they do, but for who they are; that mistakes are not shameful, but opportunities for learning; that the parent does not hold the absolute truth, but is willing to learn alongside them. In this climate, the child develops a clear identity, solid self-confidence, and a real capacity to make decisions. They are not afraid to be different, nor do they feel obligated to follow stereotypes or rigid expectations. They are encouraged to explore their dreams, express their emotions, and take ownership of their choices. Thus, they become an adult capable of managing their life with balance, building authentic relationships, and contributing to healthy communities.

This emotional maturity is also reflected in the network of friends the child will form. Raised in an environment where differences are respected and vulnerability is permitted, they will seek relationships based on sincerity, reciprocity, and emotional safety. They will know how to set boundaries, communicate clearly, and offer support without losing themselves. They will avoid toxic relationships—not because they won't encounter them, but because they will recognize the signs and have the courage to withdraw. In their circle of friends, they will bring light, understanding, and authenticity—not out of a need to be a savior, but from a genuine capacity to be present.

On a professional level, the child-turned-adult will have a healthy relationship with work and success. They will not seek external validation at any cost but will pursue their goals with clarity and discernment. They will know how to collaborate, to listen, and to assert themselves without aggression. They will have the courage to say "I don't know" and learn, to make mistakes and rise again. They will be capable of reconfiguring their professional path without feeling like a failure, because they learned from a young age that life is not a straight line, but a succession of choices and adjustments.

In romantic relationships, the consequences are perhaps most visible. A child raised with mature love will know how to love without controlling, to involve themselves without dissolving, and to be vulnerable without fear. They will seek partners who respect their rhythm, offer them space, and communicate openly. They will not confuse love with dependency, or with self-sacrifice. They will know how to build relationships based on reciprocity, trust, and mutual growth. And, perhaps most importantly, they will know how to withdraw from relationships that do not honor them, without feeling that their self-worth is diminished.

All these consequences are not guaranteed, but they are much more likely when a child grows up in an environment where love is not conditional, where the parent does not impose but accompanies, and where a mistake is not punished but understood. It is like caring for a flower: you don't just settle for watering it; you offer it fertile soil, light, warmth, and space. And when its roots need more room, you change its pot—not because it no longer fits, but because you want to see it grow, bloom, and become what it is meant to be.

The relationship between parent and child, when built on emotional maturity and authentic love, becomes a sacred space—a place where the child learns what it means to be seen, heard, and accepted. It is not a relationship of superiority, but of accompaniment. The parent does not position themselves above, but beside. They do not come with definitive answers, but with open questions. They do not impose; they support. And the child, feeling safe, dares to show themselves as they are: with joys, fears, dreams, and hesitations.

This relationship is not built all at once, but day by day, through small and constant gestures: a look that says "I see you," a question that does not judge, a hug that asks for nothing in return. It is a relationship nourished by presence, not perfection. The parent does not have to be flawless, but sincere. They do not need to have all the answers, but the willingness to search together. In this climate, the child learns that love is not conditioned by performance, but is offered unconditionally—and it is precisely this love that makes them grow free, not constrained.

As the child develops, the relationship transforms. From protection, it moves to trust; from guidance, to autonomy. The parent becomes an internal landmark, not just an external voice. The child builds their friendships using this primary bond as a model: they will seek people who respect them, listen to them, and do not reduce them to a label. They will know how to offer support without canceling themselves out, to ask for help without shame, and to set boundaries without aggression.

In romantic relationships, this foundation will be felt deeply. The adult child will know how to love without controlling, to be vulnerable without fear, and to build a relationship based on reciprocity and common growth. They will know that love does not mean possession, but shared freedom. They will know they can be themselves without losing the connection with the other.

The relationship with the parent thus becomes a living model—not an idealized one, but one that is truly lived. It is a source of inspiration, balance, and trust. It is the place from which the child sets out into the world with strong roots and open wings. And, perhaps most beautiful of all, it is the relationship that, once built with care, is not lost but transformed: from dependency into friendship; from guidance into complicity; from authority into mature love.

In a mature and conscious framework, the relationship between parents is founded on love, respect, understanding, and mutual appreciation. It is not an idealized relationship, devoid of conflict, but one in which conflicts are viewed as opportunities for growth, not as threats. Parents do not fear having different opinions, but they know how to express them without aggression, without sarcasm, and without the desire to dominate. They learn to stop before the tension escalates, to breathe, to rephrase, and to seek solutions together. They do not fight to be right, but to keep the relationship intact. In difficult moments, they do not seek validation outside the couple, nor do they appeal to the subjective opinions of family members—which can amplify the conflict—but instead choose to remain in their common space, to listen, to understand, and to reconnect.

This dynamic offers the child a living model of a healthy relationship. They see that love does not mean the absence of conflict, but the capacity to manage it with maturity. They learn that differences are not dangers, but sources of learning; that respect is not lost in tense moments, but is reaffirmed by the way parents choose to treat one another. They learn that appreciation is not reserved only for festive moments, but is manifested in small gestures, in looks, and in simple words that say: "Thank you for being here, even when it's hard."

In such an environment, the child not only feels safe but learns what a mature relationship looks like. They will know, later on, how to build partnerships based on dialogue, not competition. They will know how to stop before hurting, how to seek solutions instead of culprits. They will know that love does not fall apart in the face of conflict, but can be strengthened by how that conflict is navigated.

In a healthy relationship, parents understand that their role is to protect the child's emotional space, not to turn it into a battlefield. When conflicts arise, they do not use their children as mediators, confidants, or allies. They do not burden them with tensions that do not belong to them and do not ask them to take sides. Moreover, they carefully avoid undermining the authority or image of the other parent in front of the child—not through sharp words, irony, or comparisons, but through the conscious choice to preserve the other's dignity. They know that every attack on the partner is, indirectly, an attack on the child's equilibrium. They choose to manage their conflicts between themselves, with discretion and maturity, offering the child a model of a relationship where respect is never lost, even in tense moments.

When parents face a potential conflict with another person—whether a friend, a family member, or a school teacher—they choose to express their concerns in a balanced way, with an optimistic and polite tone. They do not turn the discussion into a moment of gossip or irony, they do not use sarcasm as a weapon, and they do not project their frustrations onto the child. They know that every word spoken in the child's presence contributes to how the child perceives the world, people, and relationships. Therefore, they choose to speak with care, preserving the dignity of the other and offering the child a nuanced perspective that does not distort reality. Instead of saying "your teacher is unfair," they might say "I think it was a difficult situation, but perhaps we can understand better what happened." Thus, the child learns that it is normal for tensions to exist, but also that they can be approached with calm, empathy, and discernment, without turning people into villains.

Children are encouraged to choose their profession out of vocation, not out of obligation, inheritance, or the desire for quick gain. They are guided to listen to their inner calling, to discover their passions, and to build their professional path in accordance with what fulfills them. Financial gains are not ignored, but they do not become the primary goal; they appear as a natural consequence of work done with dedication, not as an exclusive motivation. When the emphasis falls only on money, a wrong attitude sets in: the child learns to think in terms of profit, not meaning—of efficiency, not value. They focus on what they must do to earn and forget to ask who they want to become. Thus, the chance to develop authentic skills, to learn from mistakes, and to build a professional identity that reflects their own personal development is lost. In a healthy environment, parents cultivate the idea that work is not just a means of making a living, but also a space for expression, contribution, and inner growth.

Children raised in a healthy environment learn that popularity and prestige are not goals in themselves, but natural results of work, perseverance, and character. They understand that standing out does not mean seeking attention at any cost, but building a reputation over time based on deeds, real contributions, and the way they treat others. From their parents, they learn to distinguish between notoriety gained through negative behaviors (arrogance, superficiality, gratuitous provocation) and authentic recognition, which comes from respect earned over time. Thus, they are not seduced by the false image of instant success, but understand that true influence is built through constant effort, integrity, and the ability to remain faithful to personal values. In a world where visibility seems to matter more than content, these children grow up with discernment and a solid internal compass.

Children raised in healthy environments learn that nothing valuable is owed to them "by default"—that success, fulfillment, and respect are earned through effort, involvement, and perseverance. They do not expect everything to be handed to them without lifting a finger; instead, they understand that work is a form of respect toward oneself and others. They do not place their happiness in the hands of others, nor do they blame circumstances or people for what they have not achieved; they take responsibility for their own path. They learn that the results of their work are not guaranteed, but they are deserved, and that true satisfaction comes from the process, not just the reward. Thus, they develop into adults who do not run from challenges, do not demand unearned privileges, and do not live with the feeling that the world owes them something. They live with dignity, balance, and a profound understanding of personal value built through effort.

Children raised in healthy environments understand that learning is not an obligation imposed from the outside, but an internal process of discovery, growth, and the refinement of their own abilities. They do not view academic performance as an unhealthy competition fueled by constant comparisons with classmates or friends, but as an opportunity to contribute actively to their own development. They understand that every bit of progress, no matter how small, is a personal victory, not a trophy to be shown to others. They are not motivated by the fear of failure or the desire to be "the best," but by curiosity, the desire to understand the world, and to push their own limits. Thus, learning becomes an act of responsibility toward oneself, not a struggle for external validation. In such a framework, the child learns to enjoy the process, not just the result, and to build a healthy relationship with effort, mistakes, and progress.

Children who grow up in a healthy environment, where they are respected, listened to, and guided with gentleness, develop solid self-respect, a clear identity, and an internal compass that helps them navigate the world with discernment. They do not feel the need to validate themselves through negative social circles; they are not attracted to deviant or delinquent behaviors because they have no emotional voids to fill and no unhealed wounds pushing them toward rebellion. They understand who they are, what matters to them, and what kind of people they want to have around them. They are not seduced by false promises, superficial models, or social pressures, because they learned at home that value is not measured in appearances, but in choices. Thus, the risk of venturing into unhealthy circles decreases considerably—not because they are controlled, but because they are balanced. They choose with a clear mind and a whole heart.

In a healthy family, there are no secrets between parents and children that hide shame, pain, fears, or trauma. A climate of trust is cultivated where every member feels free to speak about what weighs on them, without fear of judgment or rejection. At the same time, a clear distinction is made between privacy—that personal, inner space that belongs to each individual and deserves respect—and secrets that isolate, burden the soul, and can generate emotional ruptures. Privacy is a right, a sign of autonomy and maturity. A secret, however, is often a painful form of protection that hides suffering and hinders healing. In a balanced family environment, the child learns that they can keep thoughts, dreams, and desires to themselves, but that they do not have to carry overwhelming burdens alone. Parents become safe spaces, not just authorities, and the relationship is built on sincerity, not appearances. Thus, the child grows up with the conviction that the truth is not dangerous, but liberating.

Parents who want children out of a pure desire born of love—and not out of personal needs or social pressures—raise free children. They do not project unrealistic expectations onto them, they do not transform them into extensions of their own identity, and they do not cultivate dependency, whether emotional, material, or financial. On the contrary, they encourage them to become autonomous, to build their own path, to take ownership of their decisions, and to manage their lives responsibly. These children grow up with the confidence that they can succeed through their own strength, that they can ask for help without becoming dependent, and that they can love without losing themselves. Parental love is not possessive, but generous; it does not say "stay beside me," but "go forward, I am here if you need me." Thus, balanced adults are formed, capable of building healthy relationships, supporting themselves, and living with dignity, without seeking in their parents a perpetual crutch, but rather a warm yet non-intrusive presence.

Parents who desire children out of pure love understand that their role is not to be indispensable, but to be formators. They do not raise their children to keep them close, but to release them with confidence, balance, and dignity. They understand that life is unpredictable, that death is a certainty rather than a threat, and that their mission is not to be eternal, but to leave behind a being capable of living and healing in their absence. They do not run from this truth, nor do they hide it under uncomfortable silences; instead, they gently integrate it into the child's education. They teach them that love does not disappear with physical presence, but transforms into memories, lessons, and inner strength.

These parents do not cultivate dependency, but autonomy. They do not raise children who will collapse in their absence, but people who can say: "I miss you, but I can go on." They teach them to manage their emotions, to build support systems, and to develop critical thinking and adaptability. They offer not just love, but tools: how to make decisions, how to rise after failure, how to ask for help without shame, and how to find oneself in moments of loss. They convey that life is not easy, but that they have, within their very being, everything they need to live it with meaning.

In this way, the child becomes not only autonomous but deeply anchored in themselves. They do not live with the fear of loss, but with the confidence that they can carry forward what they have received. And the parent, even if one day they are no longer there, will remain present in the child's choices, in their values, in the way they love, and in the way they rise. This is what it means to be a parent: to be a foundation, not a wall; to be a source, not an anchor; to be an imprint that does not weigh down, but uplifts.

Ana and Vlad met late in life, after each had carried their childhood like a wound hidden beneath the skin. Ana had grown up in a small apartment where every day was a struggle for peace. Her mother criticized her constantly, and her father, when not absent, was furious. Vlad, in turn, had been raised by a single mother, overwhelmed by worries, who poured out her frustrations on him with harsh words and long silences.

When they fell in love, they felt that, finally, someone saw them. But love was not enough to heal everything. The first months of living together were tense: Ana would withdraw into silence at the first sign of conflict, and Vlad would raise his voice without realizing it. They were on the verge of reproducing exactly what they had learned.

They started couple's therapy not because they wanted to break up, but because they wanted to not lose each other. There, they learned to look at their past not as a shame, but as an inheritance they could choose not to pass on. They understood that they could not change what had happened to them, but they could change what they chose to offer moving forward.

When their daughter, Mara, was born, they made a pact: to raise her in an environment where her voice mattered. They learned to listen to her, to encourage her, and to let her make mistakes without humiliating her. They chose not to turn her into a repair project for their own childhoods, but into a free person with the right to be herself.

They kept simple rituals: one evening a week where each family member says what they have felt in the last few days. They learned to apologize, to admit when they were wrong, and to not fear vulnerability. Today, Ana and Vlad do not consider themselves perfect parents. But they know they have broken the chain. And they know Mara is growing up in a space where love is not conditioned, but given.

At 19, Mara left her hometown with a backpack, a sketchbook, and a determination that came not from rebellion, but from a dream. She was the first in her family, across three generations, to choose higher education. Not because she was told she "had to," nor because her parents projected their unfulfilled ambitions onto her. But because she felt she wanted to build—not just buildings, but spaces that house stories, people, and life.

She chose architecture because, ever since she was little, she drew corners of the world where people felt safe. Perhaps it was a subtle way of recreating what her parents had managed to offer her: an environment where she was not afraid to dream.

At university, Mara felt for the first time what it meant to not carry a transgenerational burden on her back. She didn't have to prove anything to anyone. She wasn't there to repair the past, but to create the future. And on the evenings she returned exhausted from classes, she remembered the evenings when her parents listened to her with patience, encouraging her to ask questions rather than give perfect answers.

Mara was not just a young woman who had gone to college. She was living proof that healing does not mean forgetting, but transformation. That conscious love can break old chains and open new paths.

Chapter 17

Are you ready to become a parent?

„There is no such thing as an ideal mother. There is only the ‚good enough mother'."

Donald Winnicott

Being ready to become a parent doesn't mean having all the answers, but being willing to search for them. It doesn't mean having a perfect life, but having the courage to look at imperfection with honesty. It doesn't mean being "ready," but being present.

Readiness is not measured by financial stability, age, diplomas, or the advice received from others. It is measured by the capacity to look in the mirror and recognize what hurts within you; by the willingness to face your wounds, traumas, and fears—not to hide them, but to understand them. Because a child does not come to heal you; they come to be accompanied by someone who has the courage to heal themselves.

It is about understanding that life does not function like a checklist—that the decision to have a child doesn't come from a list of boxes to tick, but from an inner maturation. It is about accepting that there is no 100% perfect moment; that there will be many questions, and the answers will sometimes come late. Some answers will never come at all, and yet, you will keep going.

It is about flexibility. About the capacity to adapt to new, unforeseen, and sometimes painful situations. About learning to be there even when you don't know what to do. About staying connected even when you feel lost. About offering love even when you receive no gratitude.

The information and theories read before becoming a parent are useful, but they are not absolute. They can be landmarks, but not definitive maps. Every child is unique. Every parent-child relationship is a new territory discovered step by step. And no one holds the universal key.

Being ready means recognizing painful inheritances and consciously choosing not to pass them on. To break the chain. To change the pattern. To create a space where your child is not an extension of your traumas, but a free, loved, and seen being. It is about adapting everything to who you truly are, not to who you were taught to be.

It is about learning to find yourself in the role of a parent without losing yourself as a human being. Not to dissolve into sacrifice, but to rebuild yourself in balance. To understand that caring for the child does not exclude caring for yourself. That the love offered should not come from a void, but from a place of fullness.

It is about learning to say "I don't know" without shame. To ask for help without guilt. To make mistakes without condemning yourself. To repair without punishing yourself. It is about learning to be vulnerable, authentic, and human.

And perhaps most importantly: it is about learning to be there. With all that you are. With your fears, your hopes, your limitations, and your imperfect love. Because a child does not need a perfect parent. They need a present parent.

Bringing a child into the world should be, in essence, an act of love. Not idealized, romantic love, but conscious, mature love that does not seek to fill voids, but to share a sense of fullness. The pure desire to become a parent does not come from a need for belonging, social validation, or "doing what is expected," but from a profound impulse to create space for another being—to accompany them in their becoming, without conditioning them to repair something within you.

When the motivation is pure, the child does not become a project, an extension of the ego, a solution for loneliness, or a replica of one's own childhood. They become a free being, growing in an environment where love is not transactional, but offered unconditionally. And this love becomes the foundation upon which their emotional autonomy is built—their ability to feel safe in the world, to express themselves without fear, and to love without losing themselves.

Children raised in such environments are not necessarily shielded from pain, but they learn to manage it without denying it. They learn that vulnerability is not a weakness, but a bridge. They learn that they can be accepted even when they make mistakes, that they can be seen even when they do not shine. And this internal model, once formed, will reactivate in their future relationships—with partners, with their own children, and with the world.

Becoming a parent is one of the most profound choices a human being can make. It is not a decision to be taken in haste, out of impulse, or social pressure. It is a choice that demands introspection, honesty, and courage. And if your motivation does not fall within the ten unhealthy reasons described in this book—such as the fear of loneliness, the desire to save a relationship, or the need to give meaning to your own life—then, in a way, you are already on the right track. Not because you have all the answers, but because you have started to ask the right questions.

Unhealthy motivations are not just errors in thinking; they are reflections of unhealed wounds. They transform the child into an instrument of solace, compensation, or validation. But a child is not a bandage, nor a solution, nor a guarantee. They are a being with their own needs, their own path, who deserves to be seen and loved for who they are, not for what they can "resolve" in the parent's life. Recognizing these motivations and excluding them from the decision to become a parent is an act of profound emotional responsibility.

Being on the right track does not mean you are completely prepared. There is no magic moment where all plans are aligned, all fears gone, and all answers known. Real preparation is not a final state, but a continuous process. It is the willingness to learn as you go, to adapt, to recognize when you are wrong, and to repair. It is the ability to remain present even in chaos, to be honest even in uncertainty, and to love even in imperfection.

This readiness is more valuable than any theory or plan. It means you can assume the role of a parent not as a function, but as a relationship; that you can face your own limits without projecting them onto the child; that you can learn to be there—not just physically, but emotionally—with patience, openness, and humanity. It means accepting that you will not be a perfect parent, but you will be an authentic one.

Excluding unhealthy motivations does not mean you will not have moments of doubt, exhaustion, or fear. But it means you will not ask the child to resolve them for you. It means you will have the courage to carry them yourself, to understand them, and to transform them. This creates a safe space for the child—a space where they do not have to be anyone other than themselves. A space where they can learn, make mistakes, feel, and grow.

A healthy motivation for bringing a child into the world does not come from social pressure, the need for validation, or the desire to fill an inner void. It comes from love. From a profound, pure desire to share life with a new being, to accompany them in their becoming, rather than molding them according to your own unfulfilled needs. When the decision to have a child is born from a space of inner balance, emotional maturity, and authenticity, it creates the foundation for an environment where the child can grow up free, seen, and loved.

A child raised in love—not in control, fear, or projections—has the chance to become an autonomous adult with a clear identity and solid emotional balance. Love does not mean permissiveness, but presence. It does not mean idealization, but acceptance. It is that space where the child learns they can make mistakes without being rejected, feel without being shamed, and be themselves without being compared.

This conscious love becomes an internal model that the child will repeat in their future relationships. They will know what a healthy connection looks like, how emotional safety feels, and how mutual respect is built. They will know they do not have to erase themselves to be loved, nor conform to be accepted. They will know that true love does not demand self-sacrifice, but cultivates the self.

Having a child out of love is not just an act of biological creation, but one of relational creation. It is the beginning of a story where you, as a parent, are not the absolute author, but the co-creator of a space where another being can flourish. And this flourishing begins with your intention—with the motivation from which you choose to become a parent.

Ultimately, the conscious choice to become a parent is a commitment to evolution—not just the child's, but your own. It is a promise that you will continue to know yourself, to heal, and to rebuild. That you will learn to be a guide, not a master; a support, not a burden; a mirror, not a projector. And that you will learn, day after day, to love without conditioning, to accompany without controlling, and to grow together with your child.

Because, in the end, there are no perfect parents. There are only available parents. Available to transform, to question, to doubt, and to repair themselves. And if your choice to become a parent comes from a pure, conscious, and mature space, and not from the ten unhealthy motivations, then you already possess one of the most important qualities: the capacity to truly be there.

Being a parent does not mean being flawless. It does not mean having only strengths, never making mistakes, or having answers for everything. Being a parent means, first and foremost, accepting yourself with everything you are—with both your light and your shadows, with your inner resources as well as your limitations. It is perfectly okay to admit that you have weaknesses. It is healthy to know them, to understand them, and to integrate them into the way you relate to your child.

Self-confidence does not come from perfection, but from authenticity. It grows from the capacity to see yourself clearly, to know who you are and what you can offer. When you know your inner resources—patience, empathy, the ability to listen, to self-regulate, or to ask for help—you know what to turn to in difficult moments. You don't get lost in the chaos; instead, you look within for what you already possess. You don't react automatically; you choose consciously how to respond.

This self-acceptance is essential in the relationship with a child. A child does not need a parent hiding behind a mask of absolute competence. They need a parent who knows how to say, "I don't know," "I made a mistake," or "I'll try again." They need a living model, not a statue—someone who acknowledges their vulnerability and transforms it into strength.

When you accept yourself, you convey to your child that they can accept themselves as well. You teach them that they don't have to be perfect to be loved. That they can make mistakes without being rejected. That they can ask for help without being ashamed. Your self-acceptance becomes the foundation for their acceptance. In this space, growth is not a struggle, but a collaboration.

To be prepared for parenthood means, among other things, to know yourself. It means knowing what triggers you, what calms you, what recharges you, and what exhausts you. It means knowing when you need a break, when you need support, and when you need to reconnect with yourself. It is about not losing yourself in the role, but finding yourself within it—not canceling your identity, but allowing it to transform.

All the ideas explored—from self-acceptance to trusting your inner resources and having the courage to be authentic—are found in the profound essence of **The Declaration of Self-Esteem** by **Virginia Satir**. Her words, *"I am Me... and I am okay,"* synthesize with moving clarity what it means to see, accept, and love yourself authentically. As parents, this ownership of our identity becomes the bedrock upon which the relationship with our child is built. Only when we acknowledge our uniqueness and give ourselves permission to be imperfect can we create a safe and authentic space where a child can learn, in turn, to be themselves.

The Declaration of Self-Esteem is not just a personal manifesto; it is an invitation to conscious parenting, where self-love becomes the very source of our love for the other.

The Declaration of Self-Esteem

"I am me... In all the world, there is no one else exactly like me. Everything that comes from me is authentically mine.

To me belong my fantasies, my dreams, my hopes, and my fears. I own my triumphs and successes, all my failures and mistakes. Because I own all of me, I can become familiar with myself down to the most intimate details, and by doing so, I can love myself and be friendly toward myself in every aspect.

I know there are certain parts of me that puzzle me and others that I do not know, but as long as I am friendly and loving toward myself, I can seek—with courage and hope—solutions to this puzzle, as well as ways to learn more about who I am.

However I look or express myself, whatever I say and do, and whatever I believe and feel at any given moment in time, I am authentically me.

If, later on, certain aspects of how I looked, expressed myself, thought, and felt prove to be unfitting, I can let go of what is unfitting and keep the rest, inventing something new for the things I have discarded.

I can see, hear, feel, think, speak, and do. I have the tools necessary to succeed, to be close to others, and to create meaning and order in the world of people and things that exist within me. I belong to myself, and therefore, I can build my own person.

I am me... and I am okay."

Reflexion Exercise: *I am Me.....and I am ok.*

I invite you to reconnect with your own worth, to recognize your uniqueness, and to consciously activate your inner resources. Draw inspiration from the declaration above, but adapt it to yourself as a parent. You may begin with: "I am who I am. I am unique. In my role as a parent, I have qualities that define and sustain me…" You can continue the rest of your own declaration as you see fit. Below, I have provided several directions to help you continue this personalization.

Ideas of Affirmations and Directions:

- What I appreciate about myself as a parent (e.g., "I am patient," "I am attentive to my child's needs").
- What I accept about myself, even if it's not perfect (e.g., "Sometimes I feel overwhelmed, and that's okay").
- What inner resources I have and can access (e.g., "I can ask for help when I need it," "I know how to reconnect with myself").
- "I have the capacity to truly listen."
- "I am present in my child's life, even when it's difficult."
- "I express my affection without hesitation."
- "I always strive to learn and grow alongside my child."
- "I am capable of creating a safe space for my child's emotions."
- "I have a sense of humor and know how to bring joy into tense moments."
- "I am attentive to emotional needs, not just practical ones."
- "I keep my calm in challenging situations."
- "I take responsibility for my mistakes."

- “I am a model of authenticity and sincerity.”
- “Sometimes I feel tired and need time for myself.”
- "I don't always have the answers, and that’s okay."
- "Sometimes I raise my voice, but I am learning to repair and reconnect."
- "I feel guilt, but I don't let myself be defined by it."
- "I have moments of doubt, but I don't condemn myself for them."
- "Sometimes I get lost in daily worries, but I return to what matters."
- "I am not always available, but I do the best I can."
- "I have boundaries and I respect them, even if they aren't always understood."
- "Sometimes I forget about myself, but I am learning to find my way back."
- "I am not perfect, but I am good enough."
- "I can ask for help without shame."
- "I know how to breathe deeply and calm myself."
- "I have the capacity to reflect and learn from experiences."
- "I can reconnect with my values when I feel lost."
- "I have empathy and I can activate it in tense moments."
- "I can offer compassion not only to my child, but also to myself."
- "I can give myself permission to feel, without judging myself."
- "I have the courage to be vulnerable."
- "I can transform mistakes into lessons."

Chapter 18

Conclusion

"To laugh often and much; to win the respect of intelligent people and the affection of children; to earn the appreciation of honest critics and endure the betrayal of false friends; to appreciate beauty, to find the best in others; to leave the world a bit better, whether by a healthy child, a garden patch, or a redeemed social condition; to know even one life has breathed easier because you have lived. This means to have succeeded."

Ralph Waldo Emerson

This book is not a manifesto against motherhood or fatherhood. It is not a discouragement, but an invitation to awareness. It does not seek to question the desire to have children, but to place it within a space of honest reflection. Because becoming a parent is one of the most profound human experiences. And for that very reason, it deserves to be viewed with lucidity, courage, and love.

Nor is it about casting blame on the context in which we grew up, or on the parents who accompanied us as best they knew how, following the models they, in turn, received. It is about understanding. It is about looking back with kindness without remaining captive to the past. About recognizing that some wounds are not ours, yet we carry them—and that we can choose not to pass them on.

This book is not an inventory of our weaknesses, but a gateway to healing. It is an impulse to speak about our sufferings, about the fears and desires that inhabit us. It is a call to progress—not perfection, but evolution. Not the ideal, but authenticity. Because only when we look at ourselves with honesty can we become better parents, more present partners, and more whole human beings.

Becoming a parent is not just a stage in life, but a choice that defines us as individuals. It is a decision that, once made, cannot be withdrawn, renegotiated, or postponed. It spans decades, imprints itself onto someone else's soul, and leaves deep traces—whether of love, confusion, or pain. Precisely for this reason, the motivation behind this choice cannot be treated superficially. It cannot be reduced to "that's how it's done," "it's time," or "everyone has children." It cannot be left to instinct, momentary desire, or social pressure.

The desire to have children can be beautiful, but also impulsive. The meaning can be profound, but also suffocating. Continuation can be a bridge between generations, but also a replica of trauma. A conscious choice can be mature, but it requires courage, introspection, and emotional availability.

It is important to understand that none of these motivations are, in themselves, wrong. The problem arises when they are not consciously acknowledged, when they are left to act from the shadows, when they become automatisms or responses to unspoken pains. A child is not a solution, not a project, not a trophy. They are a being who comes into the world with the right to be loved, seen, and respected. And this right can only be guaranteed by a parent who has truly chosen to be there—not out of fear, not out of a need for validation, not out of a desire to fix something, but from a place of maturity and presence.

This book does not condemn, does not judge, and does not offer recipes. It opens conversations. It asks questions. It creates a space for honesty. Because before becoming parents, we are human beings—with stories, wounds, and dreams. And only when we truly look at ourselves in the mirror can we decide if we are ready to be someone else's mirror.

Becoming a parent is not about giving life. It is about accompanying life. And this accompaniment begins with a simple but essential question: *Why do I truly want a child?*

As I was saying, this book does not offer recipes. It doesn't tell you how to "be a good parent" in the classic sense, but invites you to redefine what "good enough" means for you. It has challenged you to look at yourself with honesty, to recognize your strengths, to accept your vulnerabilities, and to access your inner resources—not to become a perfect parent, but an authentic one.

Parenthood is not a role you play, but a process through which you transform. It is a living relationship in which you and your child grow together. It is about the courage to be present, even when you don't have all the answers. About the gentleness of saying, "I don't know, but I am here." About the trust that who you are, with all that you are, is enough.

This book was designed as an inner journey, not a parenting manual. Not as a collection of solutions, but as a space for reflection. We started from the fundamental question: *Why do we choose to become parents?*—a question that, although seemingly simple, hides behind it an entire world of motivations, fears, desires, and projections.

We explored the ten unhealthy motivations that can underlie the decision to have a child. We looked at them with honesty, without judgment, yet with responsibility. Because a child should not be a refuge, a solution, a second chance, or an imposed meaning. Rather, a conscious choice, born of love and availability.

Then, we spoke about the tendency to postpone this decision, hiding behind ideal conditions: "I will have a child when I have..."—stability, time, balance, answers. We understood that sometimes these conditions are real and necessary, but other times they are subtle forms of avoidance. There is no perfect moment, only moments in which we choose to be present.

We also opened up space for a choice that is often stigmatized: the decision not to have children. We affirmed that it is perfectly okay not to want to be a parent, as long as the choice is yours. That the freedom to decide is essential, and respect for another's choice is a sign of social and emotional maturity.

We then took a deep look at the emotional luggage that each of us brings into a relationship. The wounds, the patterns, the fears, the unfulfilled needs—all of these influence not only the couple's dynamics but also the way we relate to the idea of being parents. Becoming a parent does not mean starting from zero, but continuing with everything you are. And becoming aware of this baggage is the first step toward not passing it on.

We spoke about what a healthy motivation truly means: the authentic desire to accompany a being in their becoming, not to mold them according to our own needs. We understood that conscious love is the foundation of a healthy parent-child relationship. That a child raised in emotional freedom and acceptance has the chance to become an autonomous, balanced adult, capable of reproducing this model in their future relationships.

Ultimately, we reached the idea of readiness. We understood that being prepared does not mean being ready on every level, but being willing to learn, to adapt, and to reconstruct yourself. To accept yourself with both your strengths and your weaknesses. To trust yourself and know your inner resources, so you know what to turn to when challenges arise.

This is the journey you have traveled. Not a linear one, but a profound one. With questions, with second thoughts, with clarifications. With space for choice. With respect for every path. And perhaps, beyond any decision, with a closer connection to yourself.

This book is not addressed only to those on the verge of deciding whether to become parents, but also to those already in this role—parents who want to understand themselves better, to heal, and to transform. It is for couples who have children and feel that their relationship with them can be more authentic, gentler, and more connected. It is for those who realize that certain phrases spoken automatically, day after day, can become painful beliefs in a child's mind. It is for parents who are not afraid to ask themselves: "What am I leaving behind?", "What models am I passing on?", "What can I change?". It is for those who seek answers, but especially for those who have the courage to ask the right questions.

If you have made it this far, it means you have chosen to involve yourself. To wonder. To search for yourself. To take ownership. And that, in itself, is an act of profound love. For yourself. For your child. For the relationship between you.

References

Alice Miller, *Drama copilului interior*, Bookzone Publishing House, București, 2023.

Anne Ancelin Schützenberger, *Psihogenealogia – Vindecarea rănilor familiale și regăsirea de sine*, Trei Publishing House, București, 2014.

Anne Ancelin Schützenberger, *Psihogenealogia și rănile din familie*, Philobia Publishing House, București, 2016.

Anne Ancelin Schützenberger, *Bucuria de a trăi*, Philobia Publishing House, București, 2019.

Anne Ancelin Schützenberger, Ghislain Devroede, *Copiii bolnavi de părinți*, Philobia Publishing House, București, 2015.

Bruno Clavier, *Copii ce vor să-și vindece părinții*, Philobia Publishing House, București, 2020.

Cloe Madanes, *Strategic Family Therapy*, Jossey Bass, 1991.

Colette Fleuridas, Thorana S. Nelson, David M. Rosenthal, *The evolution of circular questions: training family therapists*, "Journal of Marital and Family Therapy", 12 (2), 1986, p. 113–127.

Donald M. Epstein, Nathaniel Altman, *Îmi iau puterea înapoi*, Bookzone Publishing House, București, 2023.

Elisabeth Horowitz, *Copilul și arborele genealogic*, Philobia Publishing House, București, 2016.

Elisabeth Horowitz, *Eliberează-te de destinul familial – Cum să devii tu însuți cu ajutorul psihogenealogiei*, Philobia Publishing House, București, 2019.

Elisabeth Horowitz, *Actele simbolice*, Philobia Publishing House, București, 2021.

Elisabeth Horowitz, *Fantomele trecutului*, Philobia Publishing House, București, 2021.

Elisabeth Kubler Ross, *Despre moarte și a muri. Învățături despre Marea Trecere de la pacienți pentru cei dragi, medici, asistenți și preoți.*, For you Publishing House, București, 2019.

Françoise Dolto, *Ce să le spunem copiilor*, Trei Publishing House, București, 2005.

Gianfranco Cecchin, *Hypothesizing, circularity and neutrality revisited: an invitation to curiosity*, "The Family Process", 26(4), 1987, p. 405–414.

Gisèle Harrus-Révidi, *Potolește-te, o să cazi*, Trei Publishing House, București, 2018.

Iolanda Mitrofan, Diana Vasile, *Terapii de familie*, Sper Publishing House, 2012.

Jennifer Freeman, David Epston, Dean Lobovits, *Terapia narativă pentru copii si familie*, Litera Publishing House, 2019.

Lisa Olivera, *Nu sunt suficient de bun*, Bookzone Publishing House, București, 2023.

Lise Bourbeau, *Vindecarea celor 5 răni*, Ascendent Publishing House, București, 2023.

Lynn Hoffman, *Constructing realities: An art of Lenses*, "The Family Process", 29(1), 1990, p. 1–12.

Michael P. Nichols, Richard C. Schwartz, *Terapie de familie. Concepte și metode*, Pearson Publishing House, 2005.

Robert Jackman, *Terapia copilului interior*, Bookzone Publishing House, București, 2023.

Thomas Schäfer, *Ce îmbolnăvește sufletul și ce îl vindecă*, Philobia Publishing House, București, 2021.

Virginia Satir, *Terapia familiei*, Trei Publishing House, 2011.

Virginia Satir, *Arta de a făuri oameni*, Trei Publishing House, 2010.

Zoltan Konya, Agnes Konya, *Terapie familială sistemică*, Polirom Publishing House, 2012.

Also by the author

Therapy Prompt Cards

- Self-Portrait – Boosting Self-Confidence
- Journal of the Soul – Self-Discovery
- Butterflies of Happiness
- Lessons and Reflections – Post-Pandemic
- Obstacles of Sadness
- Authentic Connections – The Harmony of Friendship
- Conversations with My Fear
- Overcoming Shame
- Dialogues for Us – Conflict in Couples
- Negative Messages – Rewrite the Story
- The Unspoken – Instead of "Goodbye"
- The Burden of Guilt
- The Power of the Entourage
- Game Over – Personal Boundaries
- Free Yourself from Worry
- Lady Grumpy – Free Yourself from Anger

- Parental Reflections – Questions that Matter
- Beyond Grades – Reasons Why We Learn
- Clothe Yourself in Love

Psychoeducational Games

- Conexio – couples
- Conexio – couples with children
- Conexio – grandparents and grandchildren
- Conexio – friends
- Nexis

www.ingramcontent.com/pod-product-compliance
Lightning Source LLC
Chambersburg PA
CBHW050525240926
51846CB00003B/693
9786303126388